Instead of Chicken
Instead of Turkey

A Poultryless "Poultry" Potpourri

Featuring homestyle, ethnic, and exotic alternatives to traditional poultry and egg recipes

by Karen Davis

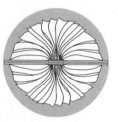

Book Publishing Company
Summertown, Tennessee

Published in the United States by:
The Book Publishing Company
P.O. Box 99
Summertown, TN 38483
1-888-260-8458

05 04 03 02 01 00 99 5 4 3 2 1

Davis, Karen
    Instead of chicken, instead of turkey : a poultryless "poultry" potpourri :
    featuring homestyle, ethnic, and exotic alternatives to traditional poultry and
    egg recipes / by Karen Davis.
            p. cm.
    ISBN 1-57067-083-8 (alk. paper)
        1. Vegetarian cookery. I Title.

TX837 .D28 1999
641.6'5 21--dc 21   99-044958

Calculations for the nutritional analyses in this book are based
on the average number of servings listed with the recipes and
the average amount of an ingredient if a range is called for.
Calculations are rounded up to the nearest gram. If two options
for an ingredient are listed, the first one is used. Not included
are fat used for frying, unless the amount is specified in the
recipe, optional ingredients, or servings suggestions.

Table of Contents

Dedication

This book is dedicated to all birds, who are so beautiful in sharing this life.

Acknowledgements

Thanks to everyone who brought their wonderful dishes to the poultryless "poultry" potluck dinners held in preparation for this book and to everyone who contributed their recipes near and far.

Consultants: Jennifer Raymond, Robin Walker, Donald Barnes, Jean Colison, Mary Finelli, Joan Holtgraver, Allan Cate, Nancy Robinson, Renee Wheeler, Lynn Halpern, Cynthia Benno

Photographers: Jeri Metz, Ken Lambert, Barbara Moffit

Illustrators: Dana Baird, Jeri Metz

Graphics Designer: Warren C. Jefferson

My special thanks to Clare Druce, Director of Chicken's Lib, Huddersfield, England, for the delightful nut roast dishes, and for creating the first organization devoted exclusively to making a better life for domestic fowl.

Introduction

This cookbook grew out of my love for food, my love for birds, and my desire for a peaceable kingdom on earth. In my peaceable kingdom, birds may be at the table, but never on it, yet they may inspire the meal in a culinary, as well as a companionable, way. The goal of this book is to show people how great a poultryless "poultry" potpourri can be. Philosophically, the idea can be compared to the substitution of bread and wine for an animal (or human) sacrifice in traditional celebrations. The principle is kept but transformed, enriched, and updated. The sacrificial altar is replaced, not by something less, but by something better. The tofu turkey replaces a corpse—let us rejoice and dig in! If bread is not literally muscle tissue and wine is not blood, few people are clamoring for a return to the "good old days." So let it be with food for all occasions as we enter the new millennium.

The culinary emphasis of Instead of Chicken, Instead of Turkey is on vegetarian recipes that duplicate and convert a variety of poultry and egg dishes in ways that satisfy the taste buds without destroying the birds. The idea for this cookbook came to me serendipitously, by "accident." One evening, while preparing macaroni for a friend's potluck dinner, I decided to throw in some chick-pea salad I'd made the night before and see what happened. The result was so delicious, I scooped this discovery into a serving dish, arranged some thin slices of Italian onion on top, and carried my prize to the party where it was an instant success. I later found that a touch of dill seed imparts a piquant flavor. This recipe makes a splendid casserole, salad, or sandwich and works well either hot or cold. The texture resembles egg salad—the macaroni has the effect of an egg white and the mashed chick-peas of an egg yolk. Made with egg-free mayonnaise, macaroni and chick-pea salad provides a tasty, high-protein alternative to traditional egg salad.

But, you may ask, why replace eggs? True, many people eat eggs thinking they are a nutritious, protein-rich addition to their meal. But when you realize that eggs are about 70% fat, that an average egg contains over 200 milligrams of cholesterol, and that eggs are frequently contaminated with salmonella bacteria, the picture changes drastically. Add to this the fact that most Americans consume too much protein, leading to osteoporosis and kidney disease, and it becomes clear that, nutritionally speaking, eggs are a liability rather than an asset.

Ethically speaking, the treatment of hens used for egg production is terrible. These lively birds are caged for life, debeaked with hot blades, and deliberately starved ("force-molted") in their cages for as long as two weeks to manipulate egg production artificially. Not surprisingly, they develop a multitude of freakish diseases including cancer, salmonella, and osteoporosis as a result of no exercise, crowding, and the stress of being unable to lay their eggs in a quiet nest.

A growing number of people are looking to free-range poultry as an alternative to this horrible system. Understandably, people think that a free-range hen spends her day outdoors, but this is almost never so. More likely, she is kept in a crowded shed with thousands of other debeaked birds whose feet never touch the ground. While less cruel than being in a cage, such a life is not truly humane for a hen, and she is slaughtered after a year or two just as her battery-caged sisters are. As egg production always involves the birth of "excess" roosters with no commercial value (half the population of chicks hatched are males), the brothers of the free-range hens are trashed at the hatchery the same as the brothers of the hens in cages.

One of the great myths of our time is that chicken and turkey are nutritious alternatives to red meat. We'll be polite and call this misinformation a "white lie." In reality, the birds who become "poultry" are forced to live and breathe in excrement, day in, day out, throughout their entire lives—not only the solid waste on the poultry house floor but the toxic ammonia fumes that arise from this waste. These poisonous fumes penetrate egg shells and enter the birds' airways and immune systems, exposing them to pathogens which are treated in turn with massive doses of antibiotics sprayed into the air they breathe and locked into their food. According to the U.S. Department of Agriculture, "Foods most likely to carry pathogens are high-protein, nonacid foods, such as meat, poultry, seafood, dairy products, and eggs."*

Who needs infested food?

On the other hand, as everyone knows, food is about more than survival or even health. It's about comfort, taste, and celebration. The recipes in this book are designed to give pleasure as well as nourishment. When I first decided to do the book, I held a series of poultryless "poultry" potluck dinners to which I invited people to bring their recipes along with their favorite dishes. The result became a tradition, as well as this cookbook. United Poultry Concerns has sponsored an open-house potluck feast on the Saturday before Thanksgiving every year since then. Often we've had a rescued turkey or two as guests of honor, along with our rescued chickens. One year a sweet turkey named Abigail joined us, resulting in a front-page story in The Washington Times. The title of the story, "Living at Thanksgiving," captured the spirit of our open house.

We always make a big platter of pasta and greens for the birds on this festive occasion. People are encouraged to bring corn, grapes, a head of lettuce, or some other treat to share with our feathered friends. Having the birds at our table instead of on it is a joy in itself. At the same time, their presence symbolizes the idea of sharing the feast and giving thanks without sacrificing appetite, abundance—or an animal!

Last fall, following nine years of operation, United Poultry Concerns moved from Potomac, Maryland, to the Delmarva Peninsula. Surrounded by the Chesapeake Bay on Virginia's Eastern Shore, the organization now has a place of its own and a lot more room. No sooner did we arrive here than we adopted eleven new hens and roosters into our sanctuary, along with a baby chicken who was rescued from the side of the road after falling off a truck on the way to you-know-where. I named her Star because she came to us as a beautiful light in the night, like all the birds whom we love so much.

Over the years, my love for birds has become centered upon chickens, turkeys, and ducks in ways I would not have dreamed of before getting to know them. The idea of chickens and turkeys as friends may seem strange to some, but for others it's a natural and delightful reality. I get letters from people from all over the world telling me, for instance, how their love for chickens is rooted in their mother's or their grandmother's love. For them, cherishing a chicken is part of the family tradition. For me, this love began with a chicken named Viva, followed by two turkey hens, Mila and Priscilla, and a handsome tom turkey named Milton. Then a little girl sent me a picture of her white hen sitting on the porch railing. She said, "Cluck-Cluck is part of our family." From that time, chickens and turkeys became part of my family, and they've been family ever since.

One thing I've learned is that no Thanksgiving Day celebration is truly complete without a turkey present, to mingle convivially with the other guests, and share the feast.

Karen Davis

Glossary

Agar flakes are a seaweed-based thickener that can be used to make jelled and other thickened foods without using animal-based gelatin.

Arrowroot is a powdered starch from the root of a tropical plant that can replace cornstarch and eggs as a thickener and binder, and makes light, tasty sauces and baked goods.

Chofu is the name I give to chickenless tofu dishes. Chickens universally adore this new name, according to recent surveys.

Dairy-free margarine contains no milk solids. Check the products sold in your supermarket or natural food store for dairy-free brands.

Egg replacers come in many forms. Check the section on "Cooking without Eggs" on page 12 for ideas on how to replace eggs in cooking and baking. Ener-G Egg Replacer (see page 10) is a convenient, easy-to-use alternative.

Flaxseeds can be ground and blended with water to make a nutritious replacement for eggs in baked recipes. To replace 1 egg, mix 2 teaspoons ground flaxseeds with 2 tablespoons warm water, and set aside for 5 minutes to become creamy and gelatinous. Flaxseeds are rich in essential fatty acids, and are one of the best plant-based sources of omega-3 fatty acids.

Nutritional yeast is flavorful golden flakes (or powder) that give zest and substance to a variety of foods. This inert yeast does not cause yeast infections. A rich source of protein and B vitamins, nutritional yeast has a delicious cheesy taste that's great in gravies, sauces, and salad dressings. Sprinkle it like Parmesan on salads, soups, casseroles, potatoes, and pasta. I carry a shaker along with me whenever I dine out. Nutritional yeast is available in natural food stores. Ask your local supermarket to carry it.

Seitan or wheat meat is a meat substitute made from wheat protein. It has been a vegetarian staple in Asia for centuries, where it is fashioned into products that resemble many different types of meat, especially poultry and beef. You can make it yourself by rinsing the starch out of a ball of flour and water dough, then cooking the remaining ball of protein in a flavored broth. By purchasing vital wheat gluten powder, you can bypass the rinsing process and just add water to mix, then simmer in broth. Ready-made seitan is also available in Asian markets and the freezer sections of natural food stores.

Soymilk is a nondairy milk made from soybeans that have been soaked, finely ground with water, cooked, and strained. Soymilk is most widely consumed in China, where it was developed as a daily beverage hundreds of years ago. Use it to replace dairy milk in your favorite recipes. Soymilk comes in vacuum packages, plain or flavored, or in a variety of dry milk powders. It is available in natural food stores and most supermarkets. Since soymilk packages don't need refrigeration until opened, they are not stocked in the dairy case, so ask where to find them. Cows and calves worldwide will thank you for making the switch.

Tahini is sesame seed butter made from ground sesame seeds and is a rich source of calcium and protein. When an egg replacement is called for, 2 heaping tablespoons tahini plus 4 tablespoons water mixed together may be used. Experiment with it in some of your favorite recipes. Tahini is sold in cans and jars, like peanut butter, and is available in supermarkets and natural food stores.

Tamari is a wheat-free Japanese soy sauce made from fermented soybeans. Use it in stir-fries and any recipe calling for soy sauce. Tamari is available in supermarkets and natural food stores.

Tempeh is a versatile cultured food from Indonesia that became available in the United States in the 1970s. Made from fermented soybeans, tempeh has a firm texture and a nut-like, mushroomy flavor, making it a desirable replacement for meat and poultry dishes without the fat and cholesterol of animal products. Tempeh contains the essential amino acids for complete protein, as well as iron, vitamin E, lecithin, and fiber, an essential dietary component totally lacking in meat and poultry. Uncooked tempeh is available in natural food stores and some supermarkets in 6- or 8-ounce packages. It also comes as precooked burgers and cutlets.

Tofu (soybean curd) is a white, cheese-like cake or block that's sold in the refrigerator or produce section of supermarkets and natural food stores throughout the country. Made of soybeans, water, and a natural coagulant, tofu is high in calcium, complete protein, vitamins, and minerals, and low in calories, fat, and sodium. Tofu is a very digestible, inexpensive, totally versatile food. Use it to replace meat, dairy, poultry, and eggs without worrying about the lactose and cholesterol found in animal products. Like poultry, tofu readily absorbs the flavor of other foods. It marinates and grills like a dream. For pointers on cooking with tofu, see "Cooking with Tofu," page 13.

Commercial Products for Replacing Poultry and Eggs

Chiken Brests™ are a fabulous textured soy product made by Harvest Direct which cook up like a chicken breast fillet. Use as is in dishes like chicken cacciatore, dredge with seasoned breading and bake, or slice into strips for stir-fry.

Ener-G Egg Replacer is a brand-name powdered mixture of vegetable starches that simulates eggs in baking. It contains no preservatives, artificial flavors, sodium, or animal products and has only 10 calories per teaspoon. Use it in recipes calling for unbeaten eggs, egg whites beaten stiff, and egg yolks. One and one-half teaspoons Ener-G plus 2 tablespoons water equal 1 egg. If your local food market does not yet carry this cholesterol-free, easily-stored shelf product, ask them to do so now, or refer to the sources on page 159. For a sample recipe using it, see "Ener-G Custard Tart Filling," page 140.

Mori-Nu Tofu is a brand of convenient, aseptically packaged silken tofu. It comes in soft, firm, and extra-firm, and either full-fat or reduced fat. The packages need no refrigeration and will keep on your shelf until you are ready to use them for making salad dressings, puddings and pie fillings, or stir-frys. Mori-Nu also makes several flavors of pudding and pie filling mixes and tofu flavoring mixes.

Nayonaise is a brand-name, sugar-free, low-sodium mayonnaise made with tofu. It has half the calories of regular mayonnaise (35 calories per tablespoon) and no animal ingredients. Nayonaise is a ready-made, delicious mayonnaise available in natural food stores and in the special sections of some supermarkets. Try it; you'll love it!

Tofu Scrambler is a brand-name mix produced by Fantastic Foods, containing a powdered blend of tasty seasonings for a wide range of quick and easy tofu dishes. Tofu Scrambler provides a scrumptious replacement for scrambled eggs, traditional egg salad, and quiche. Each box of Tofu Scrambler includes a leaflet full of recipes. For a sample recipe, see "Fantastic Chofu Scrambler," page 17.

Veganaise is another delicious vegan mayonnaise. Do look for it; it is one of the most delicious nondairy mayonnaises on the market.

Wonderslim Fat & Egg Substitute is a liquid mixture comprised primarily of prune purée and liquid lecithin. It not only replaces eggs, but is especially good for replacing both fat and eggs in baked recipes.

White Wave Chicken-Style Seitan.is a wheat-based chicken substitute that has a firm, chewy texture and poultry-style seasoning. It's a great choice for sandwiches, salads, stir-frys, and anywhere you'd use chicken or turkey.

For sources for these and other vegetarian poultry and egg substitutes, check with your local supermarket or natural food store, or refer to the sources on page 159.

Once, it was pouring rain and my mother could find neither my sister nor me. Eventually during the downfall, she discovered us holding my father's gold-handled umbrella over—that's right—Biddie.

— *Virginia Clark*

Cooking Without Eggs

In baking, if a recipe calls for only 1 egg, you can usually skip a substitute with no noticeable effect. This is often true for 2 eggs too. As the number of eggs called for increases, it becomes necessary to use a replacement. By trying out the replacements below and experimenting a little, you should get the results you want.

To hold things together in casseroles, veggie burgers, loaves:

Add a little more vegetable oil. Experiment also with tomato paste, mashed potato, mashed avocado, tahini (sesame butter), peanut butter or nut butters, moistened bread crumbs, cooked quick-cooking tapioca or quick oats.

For lightness:

Use some extra yeast or baking soda. Also use fruit juice or tomato juice to replace some or all of the liquid in a recipe. You can also use soft pastry flour instead of, or in addition to, regular flour for cakes.

To leaven, bind, and liquefy in baking, use:

• 2 tablespoons mashed banana or apricot + ½ teaspoon baking powder or 1 banana for 1 egg;

• Commercial powdered egg replacer such as Ener-G Egg Replacer. Made of refined starches, modified vegetable gums, and leavening. Use 1 to 1½ teaspoons egg replacer + 2 tablespoons water for 1 egg;

• Applesauce or apple butter. Use 2 tablespoons to ¼ cup for 1 egg;

• Commercial fruit purées such as WonderSlim and Just Like Shortenin'. Made mainly of dried plums, they are excellent for desserts, pancakes, and muffins. Use 2 tablespoons to ¼ cup for 1 egg;

• 2 tablespoons cornstarch, arrowroot flour, soft tofu, or potato starch for 1 egg;

• 2 teaspoons ground flaxseeds + 2 tablespoons warm water for 1 egg. If you have no ground flaxseed meal, blend whole flaxseeds and water in a blender for 1 to 2 minutes until the mixture is thick and has the consistency of a beaten egg.

Cooking with Tofu

As a replacement for poultry or eggs, tofu can be used straight from the package. If you find your tofu is too soft or needs some of the water removed before using in a recipe, try the following method.

1. Drain the tofu and slice into 4 to 6 slabs.

2. Place the slabs, standing up one next to the other, on a clean Turkish kitchen towel (or several linen towels).

3. Wrap the towel up over the slabs tightly, weighting the slabs down with a plate or similar object for about half an hour.

You'll now find the tofu is firmer and ready to use.

To give tofu a chewy, "meat-like" texture, you can boil it for about 20 minutes. Or you can freeze and thaw it. First, drain the tofu completely, then cut it into quarters for easy handling, and place it in a sealed freezer container or foil for 24 hours or longer. When you're ready to use the tofu, defrost it completely and squeeze the water between your palms. The tofu can now be used in stir-fries, casseroles, and marinades.

Tofu soaks up marinades and sauces, absorbing both rich and delicate flavors. Marinate cubes, slabs, or chunks of tofu in a flat glass, stainless steel, or enamel pan, turning them several times. With frozen tofu that's been thawed, mix or squeeze the marinade into the tofu.

When a recipe calls for blending tofu, it helps to mash or crumble it first unless it is very soft. Blend no more than ½ pound of tofu at a time in standard home blenders.

To measure tofu if you're going to slice or cube it, fill a 4-cup measure with 3 cups water, and float a block of tofu big enough to bring the water level up to 4 cups. This gives you ½ pound of tofu. If you're going to use mashed, crumbled, or blended tofu, crumble and measure it in a measuring cup. One cup equals ½ pound of tofu.

In recipes calling for 1 pound of chicken or turkey, substitute a pound of tofu. In recipes calling for 1 chicken breast, substitute ½ to ⅓ pound of tofu.

Breakfast
anytime

Instead of Chicken

Instead of Turkey

Fantastic Chofu Scrambler

Serves 3

Tofu Scrambler, from Fantastic Foods, will help you transform tofu into a delicious replacement for scrambled eggs. You can find it at your local natural food store, large supermarket, or through some of the sources on page 159. This is also good with rice cakes.

2 tablespoons canola oil

1 pound tofu, crumbled (2 cups)

5 tablespoons water

1 (1.35-ounce) packet Tofu Scrambler

Heat the oil in a skillet, and add the crumbled tofu. Sauté for a few minutes while stirring. Add the water and packet of Tofu Scrambler seasoning. Stir and cook for a couple more minutes, until the mixture is well blended and the tofu starts to brown.

Per serving: Calories 205, Protein 12 g, Carbohydrates 3 g, Fat 15 g

I have had a rooster for a pet for almost four years. He has the run of the house, the opportunity to be outside when the weather is good, and the companionship of a dog, cat, and humans. He knows his name, comes when called, is toilet trained, and even tries to play the guitar and piano when he sees people playing. He has great territorial sense and, when left outside, will not go near the road but stays on the property, even though it is not fenced.

— Barbara Monroe

Tofu Scramble

Yield: 3 to 4 servings

Serve this with hash brown potatoes, vegetarian sausage, and toast for a delicious Sunday brunch. For variety you can also add or substitute mushrooms, olives, crumbled vegetarian sausage, etc., for the vegetables.

Sauté the onion and pepper in the olive oil until soft.

Add the tofu, cumin, oregano, turmeric, and garlic powder, and toss until mixed thoroughly.

Stir in the chopped tomato, and simmer for another 2 or 3 minutes. Add salt and pepper to taste.

— *from Lynn Halpern*

1 onion, chopped

1 red or yellow bell pepper, chopped

2 tablespoons olive oil

1 pound firm tofu, crumbled

½ teaspoon ground cumin (freshly ground, if possible)

1 teaspoon oregano

1 teaspoon turmeric

½ teaspoon garlic powder

1 medium tomato, chopped

Salt and pepper, to taste

Per Serving: Calories 197, Protein 10 g, Carbohydrates 9 g, Fat 13 g

Chofu Rancheros

Yield: 4 servings

This is a dairy-free omelet topped with a tasty Southwestern sauce.

Omelet

1 pound tofu, crumbled

1 cup soymilk

1 scallion, minced

Rancheros Sauce

1 teaspoon canola oil

1 cup chopped onion

3 cloves garlic, minced

¾ cup sliced mushrooms

1 cup chopped green pepper

1 cup chopped tomatoes

2 teaspoons chili powder

½ teaspoon ground cumin

½ teaspoon salt

⅛ teaspoon pepper

Preheat the oven to 400°F.

Prepare omelets by combining the tofu and soymilk in a blender or food processor. Stir in the minced scallions. Lightly oil two 9-inch pie pans (glass if possible). Pour the omelet mixture into the pans, level with a spatula, and bake for 30 to 35 minutes. Loosen the omelets from the pans when removed from the oven.

For the sauce, cook all the ingredients together for 5 minutes in a covered saucepan, then uncover and cook 5 minutes more, stirring occasionally.

Place half an omelet on each plate, and cover with the rancheros sauce.

Per Serving: Calories 154, Protein 10 g, Carbohydrates 11 g, Fat 7 g

18

Shepherd's Omelet

Yield: 4 servings

You won't miss the eggs or the cholesterol either in this vegetable-filled omelet.

Preheat the oven to 400°F.

Prepare omelets by combining the tofu and soymilk in a blender or food processor. Stir in the minced scallions. Lightly oil two 9-inch pie pans (glass if possible). Pour the omelet mixture into the pans, level with a spatula, and bake for 30 to 35 minutes. Loosen the omelets from the pans when removed from the oven.

While the omelets bake, prepare the potato filling. Heat the olive oil in a large covered skillet over moderate heat, and add the filling ingredients. Stir frequently. When the potatoes are soft, turn off the heat.

Place half an omelet on a plate and cover with ¼ of the potato filling.

Omelet

1 pound tofu, crumbled

1 cup soymilk

¼ teaspoon salt

1 scallion, minced

Potato Filling

1 tablespoon olive oil

2 garlic cloves, minced

½ medium onion, thinly sliced

½ bell pepper, chopped

3 medium potatoes, finely chopped

1 large tomato, chopped

1 teaspoon soy sauce

¼ teaspoon pepper

Per serving: Calories 240, Protein 11 g, Carbohydrates 27 g Fat 9 g

Chicken Little's Favorite French Toast

Yield: 8 slices

This egg-free version of French toast is as easy as it is delicious.

½ cup water

1½ cups tofu

1 teaspoon cinnamon

3 tablespoons sweetener

2 tablespoons oil

½ teaspoon salt

8 slices slightly stale bread

Process all the ingredients, except the bread slices, together in a blender, then pour this batter into a shallow pan. Dip the bread slices into the batter, and fry on a hot, oiled skillet. Brown well on both sides. Serve with dairy-free margarine and maple syrup.

Per slice: Calories 159, Protein 6 g, Carbohydrates 18 g, Fat 6 g

Banana French Toast

Yield: 7 slices

This innovative French toast recipe makes good use of the creamy sweetness of bananas.

Mash the bananas in a bowl. Add the soymilk, molasses or maple syrup, and cinnamon. Stir well.

Soak the bread slices in the banana mixture. Fry in oil on both sides over medium heat. Serve with dairy-free margarine and maple syrup.

3 ripe bananas

1 cup soymilk

2 tablespoons molasses or maple syrup

¼ teaspoon cinnamon

7 slices whole wheat bread

— from Debra Wasserman
Meatless Meals for Working People
Vegetarian Resource Group, Baltimore, Md.

Per slice: Calories 156, Protein 5 g, Carbohydrates 29 g, Fat 3 g

Right from the start, our chicken Muffie and our turkey Mila shared a quiet bond of affection, foraging together and sometimes preening each other very delicately. One of their favorite rituals took place in the evenings when I changed their water and ran the hose in their bowls. Together, Muffie and Mila would follow the tiny rivulets along the ground, drinking as they went, Muffie darting and drinking like a brisk brown fairy, Mila dreamily swaying and sipping, piping her intermittent flute notes

— Karen Davis

Crêpes

Yield: 6 to 8 servings

You can fill crêpes with a variety of fresh fruits or fruit jams for breakfast. They also make a wonderful dessert, filled with melted chocolate and a little soymilk, or a main course, filled with asparagus and vegan hollandaise sauce.or with sautéed mushrooms. Make the oat flour by blending up oatmeal in a dry blender or food processor.

2 tablespoons egg replacer (see page 12)

1½ cups water

1 cup soymilk

1 teaspoon salt

4 tablespoons canola oil

1½ cups flour (either whole wheat pastry flour, unbleached white flour, or a mixture)

¼ cup oat flour

Place the egg replacer and ½ cup of the water in a blender, and process until smooth. Add the remaining ingredients and blend for 1 minute on high speed. If you don't have a blender, beat the mixture with a wooden spoon or whisk in a mixing bowl.

Heat an 8-inch nonstick skillet over low. Brush it lightly with oil only once, and return to the heat for a few moments. Remove from the burner, pour in 3 to 4 tablespoons of batter, and tilt the pan to coat the bottom. Pour any extra batter back into the bowl. Return the skillet to the burner, and cook until lightly browned. Flip the crêpe over and cook the other side. Stack the crêpes as you make them. Fill or wrap the crêpes with your favorite filling, and refrigerate any extra to use for dinner or dessert

— *from Lynn Halpern*

Per Serving: Calories 194, Protein 6 g, Carbohydrates 22 g, Fat 9 g

Basic Muffins

Yield: 6 giant or 12 regular-size muffins

Create your own muffin variations by adding up to 1 cup of chopped fruit, veggies, or nuts to the batter. Try using WonderSlim in these if you can; it is a wonderful alternative to using eggs in baking. You can find it in most natural food stores or through some of the sources on page 159.

Use nonstick muffin pans or spray regular muffin pans with vegetable spray. Preheat the oven to 400°F.

Mix the dry ingredients in one bowl, then combine the wet ingredients in another. Mix the two together just until the flour is moistened. Add more water, if necessary, just to clear the flour from the edges of the bowl. Bake for 20 minutes.

— *from Nancy Robinson*

3 cups unbleached flour, preferably whole wheat

1 teaspoon baking powder

½ to ¾ cup sweetener, dry or liquid

¼ cup oil and ¾ cup water
   or ⅛ cup WonderSlim
   and ¾ cup water

1 teaspoon vanilla or appropriate flavoring for your muffins

Per Serving: Calories 194, Protein 3 g, Carbohydrates 35 g, Fat 4 g

Jennifer's Pumpkin Raisin Muffins

Yield: 15 muffins

These muffins are made with a flaxseed and water purée to replace the eggs called for in the original recipe. Flaxseeds may be purchased in most natural food stores or from some of the sources on page 159.

3 cups whole wheat pastry flour

1½ cups granulated sweetener

4 teaspoons baking powder

1 teaspoon salt

1 teaspoon baking soda

1 teaspoon cinnamon

½ teaspoon nutmeg

4 tablespoons flaxseeds

1 cup water

1 (15-ounce) can solid-pack canned pumpkin (2 cups)

½ cup canola oil

½ cup water

1 cup raisins

Preheat the oven to 350°.

Mix the flour, granulated sweetener, baking powder, salt, baking soda, cinnamon, and nutmeg together, and set aside. Process the flaxseeds and water in a blender for 1 to 2 minutes, until the mixture is thick and has the consistency of beaten egg white. Add to the dry ingredients, along with the pumpkin, oil, ½ cup water, and raisins. Mix until just combined.

Fill oiled muffin cups just below the top of the pan. Bake for 25 to 30 minutes until the tops of the muffins bounce back when pressed lightly. Remove from the oven and let stand for 1 to 2 minutes; this facilitates the removal of the muffins from the pan. Remove the muffins and place on a rack to cool. Store in an airtight container.

— *from Jennifer Raymond*

Per muffin: Calories 268, Protein 3 g, Carbohydrates 45 g, Fat 8 g

Eggless Banana Pancakes

Yield: 2 servings

Be sure to use long-cooking rolled oats for these and not instant oatmeal. You can also add raisins, blueberries, or chopped apples to the batter.

Mix all the ingredients together in a bowl. Pour the batter into an oiled, preheated frying pan. Fry over low heat on one side until done, then flip over and fry on the other side.

— by Debra Wasserman
Meatless Meals for Working People

½ cup rolled oats

½ cup flour

½ cup cornmeal

1 tablespoon baking powder

1½ cups water

2 to 3 bananas, sliced or mashed

Per serving: Calories 440, Protein 11 g, Carbohydrates 92 g, Fat 3 g

Yummy Pancakes

Yield: 8 to 10 pancakes

These are simple to make and simply delicious.

Sift the flour, baking powder, and salt together. Mix in the oil and apple juice. The batter should be like thick cream, not runny. Cook the pancakes on a preheated skillet. Flip when bubbles begin to form all over the tops of the pancakes. Serve with maple syrup.

1½ cups flour

2 teaspoons baking powder

⅛ teaspoon salt

2 tablespoons canola oil

1½ cups apple juice

Per pancake: Calories 127, Protein 3 g, Carbohydrates 20 g, Fat 3 g

Blueberry Muffins

Yield: 12 muffins

Other fruit may be substituted for the blueberries.

2 ripe bananas, mashed

⅓ cup dairy-free margarine

2 tablespoons molasses

2 tablespoons cornstarch

2 cups whole wheat flour

1½ teaspoons baking soda

½ teaspoon cinnamon

¼ teaspoon nutmeg

1 cup applesauce

½ cup water

1 cup blueberries

Preheat the oven to 350°.

Cream together the bananas, margarine, and molasses in a large bowl. Add the remaining ingredients and mix well. Pour into lightly oiled muffin pans, and bake for 25 minutes. Cool the pans on a rack before removing the muffins.

— from Debra Wasserman,
Vegetarian Resource Group, Baltimore, Md.

Per muffin: Calories 127, Protein 2 g, Carbohydrates 20 g, Fat 5 g

Cloud was a very sweet, gentle hen
who endeared herself to everyone.

— Kay Bushnell

Lady Pin Feather's Banana Muffins

Yield: 12 muffins

Be sure to use long-cooking rolled oats for these and not instant oatmeal.

Preheat the oven to 350°.

Combine all the ingredients and mix thoroughly.

Spoon the batter into an oiled muffin pan and bake for 25 minutes. Cool the pans before removing the muffins.

2 cups well-mashed ripe bananas

5 teaspoons almond or peanut butter

3 cups rolled oats

¼ teaspoon allspice

¼ teaspoon cinnamon

2 teaspoons baking powder

1 cup raisins

Per muffin: Calories 193, Protein 6 g, Carbohydrates 31 g, Fat 5 g

Top-of-the-Morning Tofu Biscuits

Yield: 12 biscuits

Try these with one of the dairy-free gravies on pages 44, 79, or 153.

1 cup unbleached white flour

1 cup whole wheat flour

2 teaspoons baking powder

¼ teaspoon salt

3 tablespoons canola oil

½ cup water

½ cup soft tofu

Preheat the oven to 425°.

Combine the flours, baking powder, and salt in a bowl. Mix in the oil with a pastry blender or whisk. Process the water and soft tofu in a blender or food processor until smooth, then add to the flour mixture to form a dough. Roll out the dough on a floured surface, handling it as little as possible. Cut with a biscuit cutter, and place the biscuits on an unoiled cookie sheet. Bake for 15 minutes.

Per biscuit: Calories 105, Protein 3 g, Carbohydrates 14 g, Fat 3 g

Before the barn door crowing
The cock by hens attended,
His eyes around him throwing,
Stands for a while suspended;
Then one he singles from the crew,
And cheers the happy hen,
With how do you do, how do you do,
And how do you do again.

— John Gay

Flaky Drop Biscuits

Yield: 12 biscuits

These quick, sweet biscuits are the perfect match for your favorite jam or jelly.

Preheat the oven to 450°.

Mix the flours, sugar, baking powder, baking soda, and salt together. Cut in the margarine or oil with a pastry blender or whisk. Pour the soymilk into the dry mixture, and combine until the dough forms into a very soft ball.

Drop by spoonfuls onto an ungreased cookie sheet. Bake for 10 to 12 minutes.

2½ cups whole wheat flour

½ cup soy flour

2 tablespoons sugar

2 teaspoons baking powder

1 teaspoon baking soda

Pinch of salt

½ cup dairy-free margarine or canola oil

½ cup soymilk

Per biscuit: Calories 175, Protein 4 g, Carbohydrates 20 g, Fat 8 g

One of the most touching things about Viva, the chicken, was her voice. She would always talk to me with her frail "peep peep" which never got any louder and seemed to come from somewhere in the center of her body which pulsed her tail at precisely the same time. Also, rarely, she gave a little trill. Often I would sit talking to her, stroking her beautiful back and her feet that were so soft between the toes and on the bottoms, and she would carry on the dialogue with me, her tail feathers twitching in a kind of unison with each of her utterances.

— Karen Davis

Benevolent Banana Nut Bread

Yield: 9 servings

This recipe freezes well and can even be made without the egg replacer. Pistachios are very good in this.

Preheat the oven to 350°F.

Combine the egg replacer and water in a small bowl, and set aside. Sift together the flour, baking powder, and salt. Beat the shortening in a mixing bowl for about 2 minutes until creamy and glossy. Gradually add the sugar to the shortening, beating until light and fluffy after each addition. Add the egg replacer and beat until thick. Add the flour mixture and bananas alternately to the shortening and sugar. Grease the bottom of a 4½ x 8½ x 3-inch loaf pan. Spoon the batter into the pan. Bake for 1 hour, or until you can stick a toothpick in the middle and have it come out dry. Cool the bread in the pan for 20 minutes before turning out onto a rack.

3 teaspoons Ener-G Egg Replacer (see page 10)

4 tablespoons water

1¾ cups unbleached flour

2¾ teaspoons baking powder

½ teaspoon salt

⅓ cup vegetable shortening

⅔ cup sugar

1 cup mashed ripe bananas

1 cup nuts

— *from Cynthia Benno*

Per Serving: Calories 311, Protein 5 g, Carbohydrates 38 g, Fat 14 g

Sandwiches
and spreads

Instead of Chicken

Instead of Turkey

Oil-Free Tofu Mayonnaise

Yield: 2 cups

This fat-free, dairy-free mayo can be used as is or as the base for many other delicious dressings and spreads.

1 pound tofu

2 cloves garlic

1 teaspoon onion powder

1 teaspoon dill weed

1 tablespoon soy sauce

⅓ cup lemon juice

1 tablespoon sweetener

Water, if needed

Blend all the ingredients together, using additional water if needed to make blending easier.

Per tablespoon: Calories: 9, Protein: 1 g, Carbohydrates: 1 g, Fat: 0 g

Oil-Free Tofu Sour Cream Dressing

Make the Oil-Free Tofu Mayonnaise above using 6 tablespoons lemon juice and only ½ tablespoon sweetener.

Soymilk Mayonnaise

Yield: 1¼ cups

This recipe uses a more traditional technique for making mayonnaise, adding the oil in slowly while processing, but using soymilk instead of egg yolks.

Combine everything except the oil and lemon juice in a blender. Add the oil slowly and continue blending for 2 minutes after all the oil is added.

Add the lemon juice, a tablespoon at a time, and continue processing until thick. Keep refrigerated.

1 teaspoon sugar

1 teaspoon paprika

½ teaspoon celery salt

⅛ teaspoon cayenne pepper

1 teaspoon dry mustard

⅓ cup soymilk

¾ cup oil

3 tablespoons lemon juice

Per tablespoon: Calories: 75, Protein: 0 g, Carbohydrates: 0 g, Fat: 8 g

Another favorite memory of our chicken, Bette Sue, was finding the dogs and several cats all curled up together on the couch with her nestled down in the middle—she loved to be nice and warm. Often she took naps with two elderly cats either on a chair before the fire or on a sunny window ledge.

— Merry Thompson

Creamy Mayonnaise

Yield: 1½ cups

Agar flakes are a thickening agent are made from seaweed and available in most natural food stores and large supermarkets. This is a great way to learn how easy they are to use.

1 tablespoon + 1 teaspoon agar flakes

1 teaspoon cornstarch

1¼ cups soymilk

1 tablespoon vinegar

½ teaspoon dry mustard

½ teaspoon salt

1 tablespoon olive oil

2 tablespoons fresh lemon juice

Combine the agar flakes in a small saucepan with ½ cup water. Bring to a boil and simmer for 5 minutes, stirring often.

Dissolve the cornstarch in 1 tablespoon of the soymilk. Add it to the simmering agar mixture, stirring well. Cook until the mixture thickens.

Pour the remaining soymilk into a blender. With the blender running, slowly add the hot agar mixture, then the vinegar, mustard, and salt. Very slowly add the olive oil, then the lemon juice. Turn the blender off immediately after all the ingredients are added. Keep refrigerated.

Per tablespoon: Calories: 11, Protein: 0 g, Carbohydrates: 1 g, Fat: .5 g

Thick Mayonnaise

Yield: about 2 cups

This dairy-free mayo couldn't be easier. It uses ingredients everyone probably has on their shelves and makes a great sandwich spread.

Whisk together the flour and water in a small saucepan. Bring to a boil and cook for 2 minutes, until the mixture thickens. Let cool.

Pour the cooled flour mixture in a blender, and process with the salt, mustard, cayenne, and vinegar. Add the oil very slowly. Keep refrigerated.

½ cup flour

1½ cups water

½ teaspoon salt

2 teaspoons spicy mustard

Pinch cayenne

2 tablespoons vinegar

2 tablespoons olive oil

Per tablespoon: Calories: 14, Protein: 0 g, Carbohydrates: 1 g, Fat: 1 g

A man paid us a visit one day. Inside the barn he said, "I don't eat red meat anymore, but I still eat chicken and turkey." Along comes Milton, burdened by the overweight and arthritis afflicting turkeys who are bred for meat. Soon this man was exclaiming, with Milton standing attentively beside him, "I didn't know turkeys could . . ." Could what? I think what he was trying to say was be companionable.
— Karen Davis

Tofu Sour Creamy Dressing

Yield: 1¼ cups

You can add chopped fresh herbs to this to make herbed dressing, or ketchup and relish for Thousand Island dressing.

½ pound tofu

3 tablespoons oil

2 tablespoons lemon juice

1½ teaspoons sugar

¼ teaspoon salt

Combine all the ingredients in a blender until creamy.

Per tablespoon: Calories 24, Protein 1 g, Carbohydrates 0 g, Fat 2 g

Bantu's Almonnaise

Yield 1½ cups

Ground almonds make a delicious base for dairy-free recipes and are especially nice for anyone with a soy allergy.

Slip the skins from the almonds, if necessary, by covering them with boiling water and letting them cool enough to handle.

Place the almonds in a blender, and grind to a fine powder. Add the water, salt, garlic powder, and yeast. With the blender running, add the oil very slowly until the mixture thickens. Add the lemon juice and blend only until well mixed. Refrigerate until ready to use.

½ cup raw almonds

½ cup water

½ teaspoon salt

½ teaspoon garlic powder

1 tablespoon nutritional yeast

⅔ cup olive oil

3 tablespoons lemon juice

Per tablespoon: Calories 90, Protein 1 g, Carbohydrates 1 g, Fat 7 g

Missing Egg Sandwich

Yield: 3 servings

Some people think this tastes like egg salad; others insist it tastes like chicken salad. Either way, it is better for the chickens and for you!

1 cup crumbled tofu (½ pound)

1 green onion, finely chopped

1 tablespoon sunflower seeds (optional)

1 tablespoon your choice eggless mayonnaise, pp. 32-37

1 tablespoon pickle relish

2 teaspoons mustard

2 teaspoons soy sauce

¼ teaspoon turmeric

¼ teaspoon garlic powder

Combine all the ingredients and mix thoroughly. Serve on whole wheat bread with lettuce and tomato.

— *from Jennifer Raymond*

Per serving: Calories 129, Protein 7 g, Carbohydrates 4 g, Fat 9 g

Tempeh Sandwich Spread

Yield: 4 to 6 sandwiches

This makes a great imitation "chicken salad."

Steam the tempeh for 20 minutes. When it has cooled, grate it and mix it with all the other ingredients. Chill and serve with lettuce, or use as a sandwich spread.

8 ounces tempeh

2 tablespoons mayonnaise

¾ cup chopped celery

2 scallions, chopped

2 tablespoons pickle relish

2 teaspoons prepared mustard

1 tablespoon soy sauce

Per serving: Calories 149, Protein 8 g, Carbohydrates 11 g, Fat 7 g

Charlie has started laying eggs, and Chuck sits right next to her while she sits in her nest box. Once the egg is laid the proud father announces the event with a series of Cock-a-doodle-doos!

— *Merry Caplan*

39

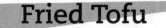

Fried Tofu

Yield: 3 to 4 servings

This is one of the most basic, yet delicious, ways to prepare tofu and is always a real kid-pleaser.

1 pound firm tofu

Soy sauce

Nutritional yeast

Cut the tofu into slices ¼- to ½-inch thick. Fry both sides on an oiled skillet until slightly browned. While they are frying, sprinkle with soy sauce and nutritional yeast.

Use on sandwiches or with mashed potatoes and gravy.

Per serving: Calories 104, Protein 10 g, Carbohydrates 3 g, Fat 5 g

In Mexico I lived next door to a family who kept a turkey in their yard. Every time I would hit a certain high note while practicing on my flute, the turkey would gobble. I spent a month playing music beside this turkey. Eventually I noticed he would stand by the fence waiting for me to arrive and play.

— Jim Nollman

Liberated "Chicken" Burgers
(Bantu's favorite!)

Yield: 4 servings

A great alternative to a chicken sandwich, full of nutritious vegetables.

Preheat the oven to 350°.

Sauté the scallions, cabbage, and carrots in the olive oil for 5 minutes, then set aside in a mixing bowl.

In a food processor or blender, mix the tofu with the flour, baking powder, seasonings, and soy sauce, and process until smooth. Add the tofu mixture to the sautéed vegetables, and mix well.

Spoon mounds of the mixture onto a lightly oiled baking sheet. Flatten the mounds to make ¼- to ½-inch round patties. Bake the patties for 15 minutes, then flip over and bake another 10 minutes.

Serve the burgers on buns with the mayonnaise of your, choice, onion, lettuce, and tomato.

½ cup minced scallions

1½ cups grated cabbage

1½ cups grated carrots

2 teaspoons olive oil

1 cup crumbled firm tofu

½ cup flour

2 tablespoons nutritional yeast

1 teaspoon baking powder

1 teaspoon "Chicken" Style Seasoning, p. 52

1 tablespoon soy sauce

Per serving: Calories 163, Protein 8 g, Carbohydrates 21 g, Fat 5 g

"Freer-Than-Free-Range" Fried Egg Sandwiches

Yield: 4 servings

Perhaps in no other recipe does tofu do a better job of replacing cooked eggs!

1 pound tofu, cut into ¼-inch slices

Nutritional yeast, to taste

Salt and pepper, to taste

8 slices whole wheat toast

Your choice eggless mayonnaise (pp. 32-37), ketchup, and/or mustard

Lettuce

Sliced tomato

Sauté the tofu slices in a lightly oiled frying pan until both sides of the slices are golden brown. Sprinkle with nutritional yeast, salt, and pepper to taste. Make 4 sandwiches using the toast, mayonnaise or other condiments, lettuce, and tomato.

Per serving: Calories 345, Protein 14 g, Carbohydrates 27 g, Fat 10 g

I never see an egg brought on my table but I feel penetrated with the wonderful change it would have undergone but for my gluttony; it might have been a gentle useful hen leading her chickens with a care and vigilance which speaks shame to many women. A cock perhaps, arrayed with the most majestic plumes, tender to his mate, bold, courageous, endowed with an astonishing instinct, with thoughts, with memory, and every distinguishing characteristic of the reason of man.

— J. Hector St. John Crevecoeur

Broth, Gravies, Marinades, and Sauces

Instead of Chicken

Instead of Turkey

Basic "Chicken" Broth

Yield: 2 to 3 cups

Use this if a recipe calls for chicken stock.

2 cups boiling water

1 tablespoon "Chicken" Style Seasoning, p. 52

2 tablespoons nutritional yeast

⅔ cup finely chopped onions

½ cup chopped mushrooms

2 teaspoons canola oil

¼ teaspoon salt

Simmer for 20 to 30 minutes. If a clear broth is desired, stain through a strainer or cheesecloth.

Per cup: Calories 87, Protein 4 g, Carbohydrates 8 g, Fat 4 g

Bantu's Brown Gravy

Yield: 2½ cups

This is delicious over mashed potatoes, stuffing, and rice.

2 tablespoons nutritional yeast

½ cup flour

2 tablespoons canola oil

2 cups water

1 tablespoon soy sauce

Per ½ cup: Calories 125, Protein 3 g, Carbohydrates 12 g, Fat 7 g

Roast together the nutritional yeast and flour in a heavy pan, stirring until they begin to brown. Add the canola oil and stir well. Then gradually pour in the water and soy sauce, stirring constantly with a wire whisk. Continue to stir while cooking until the gravy thickens.

Chunky Tomato Gravy

Yield: 6 servings

This is a tasty alternative to brown gravy, especially over Sweet Potato Stuffing, p. 114.

Melt the margarine in a medium pan. Add the garlic and onion, and sauté for 1 minute. Add the chopped tomatoes and cook until the tomatoes are soft. Stir in the cornstarch, water, salt, and pepper. Cook, stirring, until thickened, then add the parsley. Serve hot

1 tablespoon dairy-free margarine

2 garlic cloves, minced

¾ cup minced onion

5 tomatoes, chopped

1 tablespoon cornstarch

1½ cups water

½ teaspoon salt

⅛ teaspoon pepper

⅓ cup chopped fresh parsley

Per serving: Calories 51, Protein 1 g, Carbohydrates 7 g, Fat 2 g

Guinevere, our turkey, likes to be scratched gently under her wings. When she wants this attention, her technique is to walk in front of me, and flop down, blocking my movement. The sound she makes when I oblige her is an unmistakable "Ahhhh."
— Marion Cleeton

"Chicken" Garlic-Mustard Sauce

Yield: 3 cups

Don't let the amount of garlic in this recipe be cause for concern. The roasting process will mellow the flavor.

4 bulbs garlic (yes, whole bulbs and not just cloves)

1½ tablespoons spicy mustard

1 tablespoon lemon juice

2 cups water

3 tablespoons olive oil

3 tablespoons flour

Preheat the oven to 400°F.

Roast the garlic bulbs for 30 minutes, then squeeze the garlic out of the cloves after they have cooled. Combine and liquefy the garlic pulp in a blender with the mustard, lemon juice, and water.

To make a roux, whisk the olive oil and flour together in a saucepan over medium heat until brown. Slowly add the blended garlic mixture, stirring until the sauce thickens. Serve over tofu and rice.

Per ½ cup: Calories 100 , Protein 0 g, Carbohydrates 8 g, Fat 7 g

I find the dramas of the barnyard perpetually enthralling. Chickens are very sensuous creatures. They bask in the sun, languidly stretching out their wings; they revel in dust baths, stirring up dark little clouds; they are playful, even witty. Cocks are protective of their hens, and hens—well, hens are as brave as legend has them.

— Page Smith

Wild Mushroom Sauce

Yield: 2 cups

This sauce is excellent for grilled tofu. Give yourself time to prepare it because it requires slow cooking.

Soak the dried mushrooms in 3 cups warm water for 30 minutes. Strain them through a paper towel or a double thickness of cheesecloth to remove any grit and reserve the soaking liquid. Mince the mushrooms (minus their stems).

Pour ½ cup of the soaking liquid into a small saucepan. Bring to a boil and add the onion, pepper, garlic, and soy sauce. Cover and simmer for about 10 minutes. Then uncover and turn up the heat to evaporate the liquid. Add the thyme and cook until the onions start to brown. Add the vinegar and purée in a processor or blender, adding more of the soaking liquid if necessary for making a blendable mixture.

8 dried shiitake mushrooms

⅓ cup dried porcini mushrooms

1½ cups minced onion

1½ cups chopped bell pepper

3 cloves garlic, minced

1 tablespoon soy sauce

1 teaspoon minced fresh thyme, or ½ teaspoon dried, crumbled thyme

3 tablespoons red wine vinegar

Pour the blended sauce back into the saucepan, add the mushrooms and remaining soaking water, and simmer until half the liquid has evaporated, about 35 minutes.

Per ¼ cup: Calories 37, Protein 1 g, Carbohydrates 7 g, Fat 0 g

Asian Barbecue Sauce

Yield: 2 cups

This easy sauce is good as a marinade for grilled foods.

2 tablespoons sesame oil

½ cup soy sauce

¼ cup cider vinegar

2 tablespoons grated fresh
  gingerroot

3 tablespoons minced fresh garlic

1 cup orange marmalade

Whisk together all the ingredients in a small bowl, or shake in a jar. Store tightly covered in the refrigerator until ready for use.

Per ¼ cup: Calories 150, Protein 2 g, Carbohydrates 28 g, Fat 2 g.

E.R. Cope of Philadelphia reported to Dr. Kerr that his Shanghai cock was "very attentive to his Hens, and exercises a most fatherly care over the Chicks in his yard. He frequently would allow them to perch on his back, and in this manner carry them into the house, and then up the chicken ladder."

— Page Smith

Hoisin Barbecue Sauce

Yield: about 1 cup (enough for 3 pounds of tofu)

Hoisin sauce is a popular, reddish-brown dipping sauce made of soy sauce, rice vinegar, sugar, and chilies, available in most Asian specialty food stores.

Whisk together all the ingredients, and spread the sauce over slices of tofu. Let marinate for 30 minutes or overnight in the refrigerator.

¼ cup hoisin sauce

¼ cup vinegar

¼ cup soy sauce

1 tablespoon tomato paste

2 tablespoons sugar

4 cloves garlic, minced

Per tablespoon: Calories 13, Protein 1 g, Carbohydrates 3 g, Fat 0 g

"Chicken" Flavored Marinade

Yield: 1½ cups (enough for 2 pounds of tofu)

This has a hearty barbecue flavor that's especially good for grilling.

3 tablespoons hickory-smoked barbecue sauce

1 cup boiling water

3 tablespoons soy sauce

2 tablespoons rice vinegar

2 tablespoons "Chicken" Style Seasoning, p. 52

½ teaspoon garlic powder

½ teaspoon paprika

Mix together all the ingredients. Pour over sliced tofu and marinate for several hours or overnight in the refrigerator.

Per ¼ cup: Calories 19, Protein 1 g, Carbohydrates 4 g, Fat 0 g

Mustard Marinade

Yield: 1 cup (enough for 1 to 1½ pounds of tofu)

Mustard and lime make a zesty flavor combination good for stir-fries as well as the grill.

1 tablespoon canola oil

⅓ cup soy sauce

⅓ cup lime juice

¼ cup spicy mustard

3 cloves garlic, minced

Shake all the ingredients together in a jar. Pour the marinade over sliced tofu or tempeh, and let marinate for several hours or overnight in the refrigerator.

Per 2 tablespoons: Calories 38, Protein 1 g, Carbohydrates 2 g, Fat 3 g

Citrus Marinade

Yield: 2 cups

This exotic blend is especially good with tempeh.

Combine all the ingredients. Pour over tempeh or sliced tofu, and let marinate for several hours or overnight in the refrigerator.

1 tablespoon olive oil

¼ cup lemon juice

¾ cup orange juice

¾ cup lime juice

Pinch ground cumin

1 onion, sliced

Per ¼ cup: Calories 37, Protein 0 g, Carbohydrates 5 g, Fat 1 g

Chofu Salad Marinade

Yield: 2 cups

Use this to add flavor to tofu salads and other tofu dishes.

Combine all the ingredients. Pour over crumbled tofu and refrigerate for several hours before adding other salad ingredients.

1½ cups water

½ cup tamari

1 tablespoon vinegar

¼ cup crushed garlic

1 tablespoon basil

1 tablespoon dill

Per ¼ cup: Calories 24, Protein 2 g, Carbohydrates 4 g, Fat 0 g

"Chicken" Style Seasoning I

Here's an alternative to supermarket poultry seasoning. Use it to enhance soup broths, gravy, or stews.

2 tablespoons nutritional yeast

2 tablespoons parsley flakes

2 teaspoons onion powder

1 teaspoon garlic powder

1 teaspoon thyme

1 teaspoon sage

1 teaspoon celery seed

½ teaspoon marjoram

½ teaspoon salt

Measure the ingredients into a jar with a tightly fitting lid. Shake and store in a dark place.

"Chicken" Style Seasoning II

2 tablespoons nutritional yeast

2 tablespoons parsley flakes

1½ tablespoons turmeric

1 tablespoon onion powder

1 tablespoon celery seeds

1 teaspoon salt

2 teaspoons garlic powder

½ teaspoon marjoram

½ teaspoon savory

Measure the ingredients into a tightly lidded jar, and shake.

Soups
and stews

Instead of Chicken

Instead of Turkey

Chickenless Rice Soup

Yield: 4 to 6 servings

This is a good soup for children to learn how to make.

4 cups boiling water

2 cups cooked rice

¾ cup peas

½ cup finely diced carrots

½ cup diced onions

1 tablespoon corn oil

2 tablespoons flour

2 tablespoons nutritional yeast flakes

1 tablespoon "Chicken" Style Seasoning, p. 52

1 tablespoon parsley flakes

½ teaspoon salt

Combine all the ingredients in a medium saucepan, and cook over low heat at a simmer for 10 minutes.

Per serving: Calories 169, Protein 5 g, Carbohydrates 30 g, Fat 3 g

Golden "Chicken" Soup

Yield: 6 servings

This is just as healing as traditional chicken soup, perhaps even more so, as no chickens suffered so that it could be made.

Combine the water, chick-peas, onion, carrot, celery, parsnip, and bay leaf in a large soup pot, and simmer for about ½ hour.

Add the parsley, dill, uncooked noodles, and pepper, and cook 10 more minutes.

6 cups water

1½ cups cooked chick-peas

1 cup chopped onion

1 cup diced carrot

½ cup chopped celery

1 parsnip, chopped

1 bay leaf

¼ cup chopped fresh parsley

¼ cup chopped fresh dill

½ cup thin noodles

¼ teaspoon black pepper

Per serving: Calories 143, Protein 5 g, Carbohydrates 28 g, Fat 1 g.

Chicken Little especially loved tea time. Her favorite drink was iced tea, which was not complete without a jelly sandwich on the side.

— Davida Douglas

Eggless Matzoh Balls (Kneidlich)

Yield: 10 matzoh balls

What better accompaniment to any chicken-less soup than these eggless matzoh balls.

4 medium potatoes, peeled and cut into chunks

Black pepper, to taste

1¼ cups matzoh meal

Boil the chunked potatoes until soft. Mash, add pepper to taste, and cool. Add the matzoh meal gradually, and knead until firm and smooth.

Fill a large pot ¾ full with water, and bring to a boil. Form smooth balls out of the mixture, and drop into the boiling water. Cover the pot and cook for about 20 minutes. Do not overcook. Serve with your favorite soup or broth.

— from Debra Wasserman
Low-Fat Jewish Vegetarian Cooking,
Vegetarian Resource Group, Baltimore, Md.

Per ball: Calories 118, Protein 2 g, Carbohydrates 26 g, Fat 0 g

O Jerusalem, how often would I have gathered thy children together, even as a hen gathereth her chickens under her wings.

— Matthew 23:37

Chicken Mama's Special Soup

Yield: 8 cups

This is the soup to cure what ails you. It's easy to make and freezes perfectly.

Sauté the peas, chopped onion, and whole garlic clove in the oil over medium heat until lightly browned. Stir in the turmeric and water. Allow to simmer for 50 minutes, until the peas are tender.

For a thick soup: Process in a blender until smooth. Add salt to taste.

For a thin broth: Strain through a sieve. Add salt to taste.

½ cup yellow split peas

1 onion, chopped

1 clove garlic

1 tablespoon olive oil

½ teaspoon turmeric

8 cups water

½ to 1 teaspoon salt

— *from Jennifer Raymond*

Per cup: Calories 49, Protein 2 g, Carbohydrates 6 g, Fat 1 g

Spicy Pumpkin Bisque

Yield 8 servings

What a treat to serve friends and family!

1 cup chopped onion

4 garlic cloves, minced

1 tablespoon dairy-free margarine

6 cups Basic "Chicken" Broth, p. 44

2 (16-ounce) cans pumpkin purée

1½ teaspoons dried ground chili pepper

¼ teaspoon ground cloves

2 cups soymilk

In a soup pot, sauté the onion and garlic in the margarine. Add the broth, pumpkin purée, chili peppers, and cloves. Bring to a boil, cover, and simmer for 20 minutes. In a blender, purée the soup until smooth. Return the soup to the pot and heat again. Add the soymilk. Turn the heat off before the soup boils, so the soymilk won't curdle.

Per serving: Calories 138, Protein 5 g, Carbohydrates 15 g, Fat 6 g

Boyo, our turkey, took his role as guardian of the poultry run very seriously, his gobble resounding impressively around this little valley. He is now buried near the poultry orchard. We intend to plant a tree (something majestic—perhaps a chestnut or oak) in his memory. The valley seems quiet now, and we shall miss his presence.

— Clare Druce

Henny Penny's Favorite Pasta Soup

Yield: 4 to 6 servings

This recipe proves that delicious soup doesn't have to take all day to prepare.

Combine all the ingredients in a saucepan, and bring to a boil. Simmer for 15 minutes, stirring occasionally.

5 cups Basic "Chicken" Broth, p. 44

2 cups water

1 cup uncooked macaroni or shells

1 small onion, chopped

½ cup chopped celery

1 (10 ½-ounce) package frozen mixed vegetables

¾ cup chopped tomato

Pinch of oregano

Salt and pepper, to taste

Per serving: Calories 167, Protein 5 g, Carbohydrates 26 g, Fat 5 g

Chickenless "Chicken" Stew

Yield: 6 servings

This stew is delicious on its own, or it could be the filling for a delicious pot pie.

1 pound tofu

1 cup chopped onion

1 cup chopped celery

4 carrots, chopped

5 medium potatoes, cubed

4 cups water

3 tablespoons nutritional yeast flakes

½ cup flour

5 tablespoons soy sauce

1 tablespoon vinegar

¼ teaspoon thyme

¼ teaspoon sage

½ teaspoon garlic powder

¼ teaspoon black pepper

2 tablespoons dairy-free margarine

Preheat the oven to 375°.

Place the cubed tofu and veggies in an oven-proof casserole dish. Add all the other ingredients, and stir. Cover and bake until the vegetables are tender and the sauce is thick, about 1 hour.

Per serving: Calories 277, Protein 11 g, Carbohydrates 41 g, Fat 7 g

Salads

Instead of Chicken

Instead of Turkey

Tofu Eggless Salad

Yield: 3 cups

This is a good sandwich spread or dip for raw vegetables and chips.

1 pound tofu

3 scallions, minced

½ cup minced celery

1 tablespoon nutritional yeast
flakes

2 teaspoons soy sauce

½ teaspoon cumin

½ teaspoon turmeric

¼ teaspoon ground coriander

¼ cup Soymilk Mayonnaise, p. 33

Dash of black pepper

Crumble the tofu into a bowl. Add the remaining ingredients and stir well with a fork so the salad has an even consistency.

Per ½ cup serving: Calories 132, Protein 6 g, Carbohydrates 3 g Fat 11 g

Un-Chicken Salad

Yield: 3 to 4 servings

Adding fruit or nuts to this recipe will add the perfect touch for a special occasion.

Combine all the ingredients in a medium bowl, and add any options, if you like.

— *from Leslie Craine*

One (1-pound) package baked tofu, cut into ¼-inch cubes

⅓ cup soy mayonnaise

1 teaspoon vinegar

½ teaspoon Dijon mustard

½ teaspoon sugar

¼ cup finely chopped celery

Optional additions, to taste: walnuts, raisins, chopped apples, dried cherries

Per Serving: Calories 328, Protein 30 g, Carbohydrates 10 g, Fat 18 g

The little flock consisted of Reddy, Reddy's Baby, Blackie, and James, the rooster. These chickens were my friends, and I spent many hours talking to them in chicken language and feeding them special vegetables and grasses, which they dearly loved.

— *Kay Bushnell*

Chofu Salad with Parsley and Walnuts

Yield: 4 servings

This can also be served as a filling inside fresh tomatoes that have been cut in half and hollowed out.

1 pound firm tofu

1 recipe Chofu Salad Marinade, p. 51

1½ tablespoons cider or wine vinegar

1½ tablespoons olive oil

1 teaspoon spicy mustard

¼ cup minced fresh parsley

Dash of black pepper

½ cup small cherry tomatoes

Lettuce leaves for serving

2 tablespoons chopped walnuts

Crumble the tofu and marinate in the Chofu Salad Marinade for 4 hours or overnight.

To make a dressing, combine the vinegar, oil, mustard, parsley, and pepper in a small jar, and shake vigorously to blend. Put the tofu into a serving bowl, and toss in the tomatoes. Pour on the dressing and mix well. Toast the walnuts for a few minutes over medium-high heat, stirring them constantly so they do not burn. To serve, scoop the Chofu Salad onto lettuce leaves, and garnish with the walnuts.

Per serving: Calories 162, Protein 9 g, Carbohydrates 4 g, Fat 12 g

Chofu with Tahini-Curry Sauce

Yield: 4 servings

Serve this with pita bread, rice cakes, or on a bed of greens.

Crumble the tofu and marinate in the Chofu Salad Marinade for 4 hours or overnight.

Combine the mayonnaise, lemon juice, tahini, garlic, ginger, and spices in a medium bowl, and whisk well to combine. Add the scallions, carrot, cabbage, and marinated tofu. Toss until well blended.

1 pound tofu

1 recipe Chofu Salad Marinade, p. 51

3 tablespoons Oil-Free Tofu Mayonnaise, p. 32

¼ cup fresh lemon juice

1 tablespoon tahini

1 clove garlic, minced

½ teaspoon grated fresh gingerroot

½ teaspoon cumin powder

½ teaspoon turmeric

¼ cup minced scallions

1 medium carrot, grated

½ cup grated purple cabbage

Per serving: Calories 132, Protein 10 g, Carbohydrates 8 g, Fat 7 g

Moroccan "Chicken" Salad

Yield: 6 servings

Crushed pineapple makes an usual and delicious contribution to this delicious salad.

1 pound firm tofu

1 recipe Chofu Salad Marinade,
   p. 51

⅓ cup chopped unsalted peanuts

⅓ cup crushed pineapple

⅓ cup raisins

¼ cup your choice eggless
   mayonnaise, pp. 32-37

½ teaspoon cumin powder

½ teaspoon turmeric

Crumble the tofu and marinate in the Chofu Salad Marinade for 4 hours or overnight.

Combine the tofu with all the other ingredients. Serve in pita pockets or on a lettuce leaf.

Per serving: Calories 139, Protein 7 g, Carbohydrates 10 g, Fat 8 g

The cock had in his princely sway and measure,
Seven hens to satisfy his every pleasure,
Who were his sisters and his sweethearts true,
Each wonderfully like him in her hue,
Of whom the fairest-feathered throat to see
Was fair Dame Pertelote. Courteous was she,
Discreet, and always acted debonairly.

— Chaucer

Chinese Chofu Salad

Yield: 4 servings

If you can get toasted sesame oil, by all means, use it here. Even this small amount will make a difference you'll enjoy.

Cut the tofu into cubes, and combine with the barbecue sauce and marinade. Set aside for 30 minutes. After the tofu has marinated, cook on an unoiled skillet for 10 to 15 minutes.

Sauté the mushrooms in the oil and soy sauce. Prepare a dressing by combining the lemon juice, soy sauce, teriyaki sauce, vinegar, ginger, garlic, and toasted sesame seeds in a small jar; shake well.

In a large salad bowl, mix the spinach, cucumbers, and peppers with the cooked mushrooms and tofu. Combine with the dressing and serve.

Per serving: Calories 216, Protein 16 g, Carbohydrates 20 g, Fat 7 g

1 pound firm tofu

3 tablespoons hickory-flavored barbecue sauce

1 recipe Chofu Salad Marinade, p. 51

2 cups slivered mushrooms

1 teaspoon toasted sesame oil or canola oil

2 tablespoons soy sauce

1½ tablespoons lemon juice

2 teaspoons soy sauce

1 tablespoon teriyaki sauce

1 tablespoon wine vinegar

1 teaspoon grated fresh gingerroot

1 teaspoon crushed fresh garlic

2 tablespoons toasted sesame seeds

4 cups chopped spinach

2 thinly sliced peeled cucumbers

1 cup chopped bell pepper

Macaroni & Chick-Pea Salad

Yield: 4 servings

This will remind you of egg salad.

1 (18-ounce) can chick-peas, or 2 cups cooked chick-peas

½ cup Oil-Free Tofu Mayonnaise, p. 32

½ cup chopped onion

½ cup chopped celery

½ teaspoon garlic powder

1 teaspoon crushed dill leaves

1 tablespoon soy sauce

2 cups cooked macaroni

Mash the chick-peas with a fork, and mix with the mayonnaise, onion, celery, garlic powder, dill, and soy sauce in a bowl. Add the cooked macaroni and combine together.

Per serving: Calories 242, Protein 12 g, Carbohydrates 43 g, Fat 2 g

Another rooster, Benny, enjoyed riding a motorcycle around the yard with me—very slowly, of course, and in my younger days! Benny's grandson, Ko Ko, who is now eight years old, nearly blind, and almost completely deaf, once had a blind hen he protected and guided around the yard, calling her when he found goodies.

— *Barbara Moffit*

Cranberry-Fruit Relish

Yield: 12 servings

Don't miss making this at Thanksgiving. Thanks to Lola Olsen for offering her mom's recipe.

Pulse the cranberries, apples, oranges, grapes, pineapple, ginger, and pecans in a food processor until well mixed.

Bring 2 cups of water to a boil, and stir in the agar.

Stir the sugar and strawberries into the boiling water. Add the maple syrup and simmer for 20 minutes. Cool until lukewarm. Pour onto the fruit and nuts. Stir and chill for at least 4 hours.

— *from Edith Miller*

1 quart cranberries

3 crisp, unpeeled apples

3 oranges, peeled and chopped

1 bunch grapes (about 1½ cups)

1 (8-ounce) can crushed pineapple

1 tablespoon chopped fresh gingerroot

½ cup chopped pecans

5 tablespoons agar flakes

¼ cup sugar

8 large strawberries, chopped

1 tablespoon maple syrup

Per Serving: Calories 134, Protein 1 g, Carbohydrates 25 g, Fat 3 g

Main Dishes

Instead of Chicken

Instead of Turkey

Deep-Dish Biscuit Pie

Yield: 6 to 8 servings

You can experiment with other vegetables and herbs if you like.

1 cup chopped onions

1 cup chopped celery

1 cup sliced carrots

2 cups potatoes, cut in ½-inch cubes

1 cup frozen peas

1 cup frozen corn

1 pound tofu, cubed

2½ cups soymilk

3 tablespoons tamari

⅓ cup fresh minced parsley

1 teaspoon garlic powder

3 tablespoons "Chicken" Style Seasoning, p. 52, or other poultry seasoning

½ teaspoon crushed sage

½ teaspoon thyme

3 cans refrigerated dough biscuits (10 per can)

Preheat the oven to 350°F.

Steam the vegetables for 5 minutes. Combine with the remaining ingredients, except the biscuits, in a large saucepan, and cook over medium heat for 5 minutes. Press 2 cans of biscuit dough into a large, oiled baking dish. Pour the filling onto this crust. Bake for 30 minutes. Top with the remaining biscuits, and bake another 10 minutes.

Per serving: Calories 598, Protein 18 g, Carbohydrates 87 g, Fat 18 g

Mrs. Gobble-Good's Golden Brown Pie

Yield: 6 servings

1 cup flour

2 tablespoons oil

¼ cup cold water

⅔ cup lentils

½ teaspoon thyme

1 tablespoon parsley

1 teaspoon salt

½ cup chopped onion

1 cup chopped carrots

½ cup chopped celery

4 potatoes, peeled and cubed

1 tablespoon dairy-free margarine

3 tablespoons flour

1 cup water to cook vegetables

Make an uncooked pie crust for placing on top of the pie by combining the flour and oil with a pastry blender or whisk until the mix is roughly the size of peas. Gradually add the cold water until you can form a ball of dough.

Wrap the dough in plastic, and set aside in the refrigerator to chill while making the filling.

To make the filling, simmer the lentils in 2 cups of water in a saucepan on low heat until soft, about 45 minutes. Season with the thyme, parsley, and salt 5 minutes before they are done.

Put the chopped onion, carrots, celery, and potatoes in a large saucepan with 6 cups water. Bring to a boil and cook for 10 minutes. Drain and save the cooking water.

Preheat the oven to 350°F.

Make a gravy by melting the margarine in a small pan. Add the 3 tablespoons flour, then gradually add 1 cup of water from cooking the vegetables. Stir and cook until smooth and thick. Place the vegetables in a 2-quart casserole dish, then add the lentils and gravy. Stir together. If the mixture is too thick, add a little more water from the vegetables. Roll out the pie crust, and place over the top of the casserole. Bake for 40 to 45 minutes.

Per serving: Calories 476, Protein 13 g, Carbohydrates 89 g, Fat 7 g

Priscilla's Tofu Pot Pie Filling

Yield: 6 to 8 servings

This recipe is for anyone who ever loved chicken pot pie.

Filling

1½ pounds firm tofu

¼ cup flour

1 teaspoon salt

½ teaspoon black pepper

½ teaspoon garlic powder

2 tablespoons oil

1½ cups chopped onions

1 cup sliced carrots

1 cup sliced celery

2 tablespoons water

1 cup peas, fresh or frozen

Gravy

2 tablespoons dairy-free margarine

4 cups sliced mushrooms

¼ cup whole wheat flour

1 teaspoon salt

1 teaspoon sage

1 teaspoon garlic powder

To make the filling, cut the tofu into ½-inch cubes. Mix the flour, salt, pepper, and garlic powder. Add the tofu cubes and toss until coated. Sauté in a large skillet in the oil until golden and crisp. Stir in the onions and continue cooking for 3 minutes. Then add the carrots, celery, and 2 tablespoons water. Cover the pan and cook over medium heat. Stir gently every minute or so until the carrots are just tender. Remove from the heat and stir in the peas.

To make the gravy, melt the margarine in a large saucepan, and add the sliced mushrooms. Cover the pan and sauté over medium heat until the mushrooms are soft. Stir in the ¼ cup whole wheat flour, salt, sage, garlic powder, thyme, paprika, and black pepper, and cook over low heat for 2 to 3 minutes. Whisk in the 2 to 3 cups water, and simmer, uncovered, until gravy is thickened—about 10 minutes. Mix half

74

the gravy into the tofu and vegetables. Set the remainder aside.

To make the crust, combine the 1½ cups whole wheat flour, wheat germ, and ½ teaspoon salt, and stir to mix. Cut in the margarine until the mixture resembles coarse cornmeal. Add the 6 tablespoons cold water all at once, and stir just enough to form the dough into a ball. Divide the dough in half, and roll the first half out on a floured surface. Place in a 10-inch pie plate. Roll out the remaining half of the dough, and set aside.

Preheat the oven to 400°F.

Spread the tofu and vegetable mixture into the dough-lined pie plate. Pour the remaining gravy over the top, and cover with the top crust. Fold the edges of the top and bottom crusts together, and pinch to form an edge. Cut 4 to 6 one-inch slits in the top crust to allow steam to escape while baking. Bake for 20

½ teaspoon thyme

½ teaspoon paprika

¼ teaspoon black pepper

2 to 3 cups water (depending on how thick you like your gravy)

Crust

1½ cups whole wheat pastry flour

½ cup wheat germ

½ teaspoon salt

⅓ cup dairy-free margarine

6 tablespoons cold water

minutes. Reduce the heat to 350°F, and bake an additional 20 to 30 minutes, until the crust is nicely browned.

— from Jennifer Raymond

Per serving: Calories 554, Protein 21 g, Carbohydrates 61 g, Fat 25 g

Chick-Pea Croquettes

Yield: 16 croquettes

Chick-peas make a rich-tasting substitute for ground poultry in these croquettes.

2 cups cooked chick-peas,
    plus ½ cup broth from cooking

2 cups cooked brown rice

¼ cup finely chopped onions

2 tablespoons tahini

2 tablespoons soy sauce

1 cup soft bread crumbs

Salt and pepper, to taste

½ cup wheat germ

Preheat the oven to 350°F.

Mash the chick-peas with their broth. Combine with all the other ingredients, except the wheat germ, and form into croquettes. Roll the croquettes in the wheat germ, and bake for 25 minutes, turning once. Serve with gravy or cranberry sauce.

Per croquette: Calories 196, Protein 4 g, Carbohydrates 16 g, Fat 2 g

As for the hen, she is rich in comfortable sounds, chirps and chirrs, and, when she is a young pullet, a kind of sweet singing that is full of contentment when she is clustered together with her sisters and brothers in an undifferentiated huddle of peace and well-being waiting for darkness to envelop them.

— Page Smith

Notchicken and Dumplings

Yield: 4 to 6 servings

This recipe highlights the use of seitan, a meat-substitute made from wheat that has been eaten in Asia for centuries. Its naturally light flavor makes it a perfect poultry substitute.

Make biscuits by mixing the flour, baking powder, salt, and the 1 cup of diced wheat meat. Cut in the oil to form pea-size balls using a potato masher or pastry blender. Stir in the soymilk until the mixture forms a ball of dough.

Bring 10 cups of water to a low boil. Stir in the soup powder or broth mix and the poultry seasoning.

With well-oiled fingers, pinch off about 2 tablespoons of biscuit dough at a time, and drop it into the simmering water. Cover and cook about 30 minutes. Stir occasionally to prevent the dumplings from sticking. Add the rest of the wheat meat to the broth just long enough to heat through.

— *from Nancy Robinson*

2 cups unbleached flour

2 cups baking powder

½ teaspoon salt

1 cup diced "chicken" wheat meat

4 Tablespoons oil

¾ cup soymilk

3 tablespoons your favorite chicken-style broth mix (enough to flavor 10 cups stock)

1 tablespoon poultry seasoning

½ (1-pound) package "chicken" wheat meat, diced, or 1½ cups chicken-style seitan

Per Serving: Calories 408, Protein 25 g, Carbohydrates 47 g, Fat 12 g

"Chicken" Fried Steak Dinner

Yield: 4 to 6 servings

Tofu replaces chicken here to make the consummate country meal.

1 pound frozen tofu, thawed

2 tablespoons soy sauce

Salt and pepper, to taste

¼ cup flour

1 teaspoon baking powder

1 tablespoon canola oil

4 tablespoons water

Squeeze or press as much water as you can out of the thawed tofu, then crumble. Sprinkle the soy sauce over the tofu pieces, then add salt and pepper to taste, and mix well.

In a separate bowl, mix the flour and baking powder. Add the oil and water until the mixture forms a paste. Mix the paste into the tofu, and divide into 8 balls.

Cut up 16 pieces of wax paper about 4 inches square, and sprinkle each one with flour. Wet your hands and slightly flatten each ball by placing it on the floured wax paper, covering with another sheet, and pressing until flat.

Freeze the patties with the waxed paper on for at least 30 minutes before cooking. Remove the wax paper and cook the patties on an oiled skillet. Brown on each side. Serve with Oklahoma White Gravy, on the facing page, and mashed potatoes on the side.

Per patty: Calories 73, Protein 5 g, Carbohydrates 4 g, Fat 4 g

Oklahoma White Gravy

Yield: 3 cups

Now you can make a dairy-free version of delicious white gravy.

Heat the oil in a skillet. Add the flour and stir well. Slowly pour in the milk while whisking constantly, and keep stirring until a smooth gravy is formed. Simmer the gravy over low heat until it bubbles.

3 tablespoons oil

⅓ cup flour

3 cups soymilk

Salt and pepper, to taste

Per ½ cup serving: Calories 122, Protein 4 g, Carbohydrates 7 g, Fat 9 g

Mashed Potatoes

Yield: 4 servings

If the potato skins are thin and fresh, you may prefer to leave the potatoes unpeeled.

Place the potatoes in a pan, cover with water, and boil until tender. Drain the water, and add the margarine, creamer, and salt. Mash and stir until creamy.

4 medium potatoes, peeled and sliced

4 tablespoons dairy-free margarine

¼ cup nondairy creamer

Salt, to taste

Per Serving: Calories 295, Protein 3 g, Carbohydrates 43 g, Fat 13 g

Boyo's Sesame and Brazil Nut Roast

Yield: 4 servings

If you can find vegetable yeast extract (such as Marmite or Vegemite) in specialty food stores, you'll enjoy the rich, hearty flavor they add here.

1 large chopped onion

2 tablespoons oil

2 tablespoons flour

½ cup vegetable stock

1 teaspoon vegetable yeast extract, or 1 tablespoon nutritional yeast flakes

2 tomatoes, chopped

⅔ cup coarsely grated Brazil nuts

¼ cup sesame seeds

6 tablespoons bread crumbs

2 tablespoons rolled oats

1 teaspoon dried herbs

2 tablespoons chopped fresh parsley

Preheat the oven to 375°F.

Gently sauté the onions in the oil for 5 minutes. Stir in the flour and add the yeast extract or nutritional yeast. Stir until thickened.

Place the remaining ingredients in a large bowl, and mix well with the cooked onions. Spoon into an oiled 1-quart ovenproof dish or loaf tin, and bake for 35 to 45 minutes.

Per serving: Calories 388, Protein 8 g, Carbohydrates 23 g, Fat 28 g

Christmas Cashew and Chestnut Roast

Yield: 6 to 8 servings

This recipe makes use of two popular British ingredients, yeast extract (such as Marmite or Vegemite) and chestnut purée. You can find these in speciality food stores, natural foods stores, and larger supermarkets.

Heat the oil in a saucepan, and add the onions, garlic, rosemary, and thyme. Sauté until the onions are soft but not browned. Place in a large mixing bowl. Add the ground cashews, mashed carrots, bread crumbs, dissolved yeast extract, and mix well. Add salt and pepper to taste. Mix the flour into a smooth paste with a little water, and add to the cashew mixture. Combine thoroughly. The mixture should be moist, but hold together well. Combine the chestnut purée and salt with just enough water to process in a blender.

Preheat the oven to 350°F.

Oil a 2-pound loaf pan, and put half the cashew mixture in the bottom. Mold the chestnut purée into a sausage shape, and lay it lengthwise in the pan, not touching the sides. Then add the rest of the cashew mixture, and press down. Bake for 1½ hours. For best results, allow the roast to cool for 15 minutes before turning out and slicing.

1 tablespoon olive oil

2 medium onions, finely chopped

4 cloves garlic, crushed (optional)

1 teaspoon dried rosemary

1 teaspoon dried thyme

1¼ cup ground cashews

5 medium carrots, cooked and roughly mashed

¾ cup brown bread crumbs

2 teaspoons yeast extract (such as Marmite or Vegemite), or 2 tablespoons nutritional yeast flakes, dissolved in ⅞ cup hot water

Salt and pepper, to taste

3 heaping tablespoons whole wheat flour

1 cup canned chestnut purée

½ teaspoons salt

Per serving: Calories 270, Protein 6 g, Carbohydrates 29 g, Fat 14 g

Un-Turkey Casserole

Yield: 6 to 8 servings

I made this up to duplicate a little casserole I had at fantastic Kate's Joint in New York. Basically it's just stuffing, gravy, and faux-turkey, layered. This got rave reviews for Thanksgiving.

1 (8-ounce) bag crumb stuffing mix

1 large onion, chopped

2 tablespoons canola oil

½ (10-ounce) package vegetarian sausage (optional)

1½ (8-ounce) packages of baked tofu or vegetarian turkey, thinly sliced

3 cups dairy-free mushroom gravy

Preheat the oven to 350°F.

Prepare the bag of stuffing per package instructions using dairy-free margarine instead of butter. Sauté the onion in the oil until brown, and add to the prepared stuffing along with the vegetarian sausage, if desired.

Place half the stuffing in an oiled casserole. Layer the vegetarian turkey or baked tofu over this, then half the gravy. Add the rest of the stuffing, then the remaining vegetarian turkey or tofu and gravy. Bake for 25 minutes or until heated through.

— *from Leslie Craine*

Per Serving: Calories 376, Protein 19 g, Carbohydrates 50 g, Fat 9 g

Stuffed Squash (Not Turkeys!)

Yield: 6 servings

Squash is elevated to a main dish in this hearty recipe.

Combine the tofu, soy sauce, turmeric, parsley, black pepper, and garlic powder. The sauté the celery, mushrooms, and onion in the oil until just browned. Combine the sautéed vegetables with the tofu mixture, along with the bread crumbs and poultry seasoning.

Preheat the oven to 350°F.

Remove enough of the centers from the squash halves so you can put approximately 1 cup of the tofu/vegetable stuffing in each squash. Pack the squash with the stuffing, place on a cooking sheet, and bake for 1 hour. Let cool for 10 to 15 minutes before serving. Serve garnished with chopped parsley.

2 pounds firm tofu, crumbled

2 tablespoons soy sauce

2 teaspoons turmeric

½ cup chopped fresh parsley

¼ teaspoon black pepper

2 teaspoons garlic powder

1 cup chopped celery

1½ cups sliced mushrooms

1 cup finely chopped onions

¼ cup canola oil

4 cups whole wheat bread crumbs

1 teaspoon poultry seasoning

3 acorn (or other bowl-shaped) squash, cut in half and seeds removed

Per serving: Calories 351, Protein 15 g, Carbohydrates 34 g, Fat 15 g

Turkey-Lurkey's Teriyaki Tofu

Yield: 6 servings

These may be served as a main dish or with toothpicks as an hors d'oeuvre.

1½ pounds tofu

¼ cup soy sauce

3 tablespoons nutritional yeast flakes

1 teaspoon onion powder

1 teaspoon garlic powder

10 bamboo skewers

1 tablespoon olive oil

½ cup teriyaki sauce

Preheat the oven to 350°F.

Cut the tofu into strips about ½-inch thick and ¾-inch wide. Place them on a lightly oiled cookie sheet.

Sprinkle with the soy sauce. In a cup, mix together the nutritional yeast, onion powder, and garlic powder, and shake the yeast mixture over the tofu strips. Bake for 15 minutes, then flip over, and bake for 10 more minutes. Let cool. Soak the bamboo skewers in cold water for 15 minutes to help keep them from charring.

Brush the baked strips with the teriyaki sauce and olive oil, then thread on the skewers. Heat under the broiler for 5 minutes, watching carefully so they don't burn.

Per serving: Calories 160, Protein 11 g, Carbohydrates 12 g, Fat 7 g

Lemon "Chicken"

Yield: 4 servings

This easy recipe is delicious with cooked greens, a fresh salad, or as the basis for a stir-fry.

Cut the tofu into small cubes. Stir-fry the tofu, garlic, and scallions in the olive oil in a hot pan for 2 minutes.

Sprinkle the flour and yeast over the tofu, and stir-fry for 2 minutes more. Add the lemon juice and soy sauce, and stir until the liquids are absorbed.

1 pound tofu

1 teaspoon minced fresh garlic

½ cup chopped scallions

2 teaspoons olive oil

1 tablespoon flour

1 tablespoon nutritional yeast flakes

2 tablespoons lemon juice

2 tablespoons soy sauce

Per serving: Calories 128, Protein 10 g, Carbohydrates 6 g, Fat 7 g

All of my chickens, and my turkey, were fond of sitting in my lap. They would stretch out their necks to be petted, and eventually fall asleep that way, with their necks draped over my leg.

— Cindy Pollock

Chickenless Nuggets in Tomato Sauce

Yield: about 18 nuggets (serves 3 to 4)

A commercial brand of seitan called Wheat Meat makes excellent nuggets in this recipe. It's available ready-made at natural food stores, community co-ops, and some supermarkets nation-wide. If it's not yet at your local supermarket, you can order the dry mix from the sources on page 159.

One (18-ounce) package chicken-style seitan (1¾ cups)

⅓ cup flour

⅓ cup bread crumbs

¼ teaspoon salt

⅛ teaspoon pepper

¼ teaspoon Italian seasonings

⅓ cup soymilk

Olive (or other vegetable) oil for frying

One 26-ounce jar of your favorite bottled or homemade spaghetti sauce

Preheat the oven to 375°F.

Cut the chicken-style seitan into bite-sized nuggets. Mix the flour and bread crumbs with the salt, pepper, and Italian seasonings. Dip the nuggets into the soymilk and then into the bread crumb mixture. Fry the nuggets in oil until golden brown, or oven-bake on a lightly oiled cookie sheet for 10 to 12 minutes on each side. Cover the bottom of a baking dish with a layer of spaghetti sauce, and place the nuggets on top. Pour another layer of sauce over the nuggets, and bake for 20 to 30 minutes.

— *from Lynn Halpern*

Per Serving: Calories 342, Protein 27 g, Carbohydrates 50 g, Fat 5 g

Red Pepper Chofu
with Spinach and Pine Nuts

Yield: 6 servings

Pine nuts (also known as pinion or pignolia) are what is traditionally used to make pesto. Buy them in small quantities and store them in the refrigerator or freezer to keep them fresh, as you would any nuts.

Have all the vegetables prepared and chopped before you begin. Heat the oil in a medium skillet or large wok. Add the tofu, spices, carrot, pepper, and onions, and stir-fry for 5 minutes. Add the nuts and spinach, and continue cooking for 3 to 4 minutes. Stir in the lemon juice. Turn the heat off when thoroughly heated through. Serve over pasta.

2 tablespoons olive oil

1 pound tofu, cubed

½ teaspoon chili pepper flakes

1 tablespoon mild paprika

½ teaspoon black pepper

½ teaspoon salt

¾ cup chopped carrots

¾ cup chopped red bell pepper

¾ cup chopped onions

½ cup toasted pine nuts

2 (10-ounce) packages frozen spinach, thawed and squeezed dry

2 tablespoons lemon juice

Per serving: Calories 207, Protein 10 g, Carbohydrates 11 g, Fat 13 g

Cutlets "Marsala"

Yield: 4 servings

Serve this traditional Italian dish with risotto or your favorite pesto pasta.

½ pound chicken-style seitan or "wheat meat"

Salt and pepper, to taste

½ to ¾ cup bread crumbs

½ cup thinly sliced mushrooms

3 tablespoons olive oil

2 tablespoons dairy-free margarine

Soymilk, for dipping

½ cup dry Marsala wine or port

2 tablespoons chopped olives

Cut the seitan into ½ inch-thick cutlets. Add salt and pepper to the bread crumbs, to taste. Sauté the mushrooms in 1 tablespoon of the olive oil and the margarine in a heavy skillet until soft, then remove from the pan. Dip the seitan slices in the soymilk and then into the bread crumbs. Brown the seitan on both sides in the remaining 2 tablespoons olive oil. Add the sautéed mushrooms, wine, and chopped olives. Cover and simmer for 5 to 10 minutes. Remove the seitan cutlets and place on a platter. Spoon the sauce over the cutlets, and serve.

— from Lynn Halpern

Per Serving: Calories 321, Protein 13 g, Carbohydrates 20 g, Fat 18 g

Thai-Style Tofu in Peanut Sauce

Yield: 4 to 6 servings

Thai food has become very popular lately, marrying the earthy richness of peanuts and soy sauce with the zest of hot pepper. This dish is a great way to introduce this cuisine to the uninitiated.

Sauté the tofu cubes in the peanut oil until golden brown. Remove from pan. In the same pan, stir-fry the broccoli, carrots, and green onions until tender in whatever oil is leftover from frying the tofu. Add the garlic and sauté a minute more. Mix the peanut butter, Worcestershire sauce, vinegar, and soy sauce in a small bowl. Add this mixture and the tofu cubes to the vegetables. Stir and heat until the mixture is well blended and the sauce begins to bubble. Serve over steamed rice or rice noodles, and top with chopped peanuts and cilantro.

— *from Lynn Halpern*

1 pound firm tofu, cut into cubes

2 tablespoons peanut oil

2 cups chopped broccoli

1 cup thinly sliced carrots

1 cup green onions

3 to 5 cloves garlic, chopped

2 tablespoons peanut butter

1 tablespoon vegetarian Worcestershire sauce

1 tablespoon rice vinegar

1 tablespoon soy sauce

1 tablespoon brown sugar

1 teaspoon red pepper flakes

Chopped peanuts, for garnish

Chopped cilantro, for garnish

Per Serving: Calories 193, Protein 9 g, Carbohydrates 11 g, Fat 12 g

Chofu Vegetable Stir-Fry with Sherry

Yield: 6 servings

This basic stir-fry is so easy and delicious, it will become a family favorite your kids will ask for again and again.

1½ pounds tofu

3 tablespoons sherry or white wine, or non-alcoholic white wine

4 cups chopped broccoli

2 tablespoons soy sauce

⅓ cup water

1½ tablespoons cornstarch

1 tablespoon canola oil

2 cloves garlic, minced

1½ cups sliced mushrooms

6 cups chopped fresh spinach

Cube the tofu and marinate in the sherry or white wine for 30 minutes. Steam the broccoli for 2 minutes, then rinse under cold water immediately. Mix together the soy sauce, water, and cornstarch. Heat the oil in a skillet, and sauté the tofu and garlic for a few minutes. Add the cornstarch mixture, the broccoli, mushrooms, and spinach, stirring constantly until the sauce thickens. Cook for 5 minutes and serve over hot rice.

Per serving: Calories 161, Protein 11 g, Carbohydrates 10 g, Fat 7 g

Ma Po Chofu (Szechuan-Style)

Yield: 4 servings

This is the Chinese specialty dish for people who like it hot!

To make a sauce, whisk together the broth, sherry, wine vinegar, soy sauce, chili paste, and sugar, and set aside. Then stir-fry the tofu cubes, garlic, ginger, scallions, and hot pepper in the oil for 3 minutes.

Add the sauce ingredients, bring to a boil, and simmer for 5 minutes. Then add the cornstarch dissolved in water. Cook for 1 minute and remove from the heat. Serve hot over rice, garnished with chopped scallion greens.

1½ cups Basic "Chicken" Broth, p. 44, or water

2 tablespoons sherry

½ tablespoon wine vinegar

3 tablespoons soy sauce

1 teaspoon Chinese chili paste or other Chinese-style hot sauce

1 teaspoon sugar

1 pound tofu, cubed

3 cloves garlic, minced

1 tablespoon grated fresh gingerroot

⅔ cup chopped scallions

1 hot chili pepper, finely chopped

2 tablespoons canola oil

1 tablespoon cornstarch dissolved in 2 tablespoons water

Per serving: Calories 234, Protein 9 g, Carbohydrates 20 g, Fat 11

Stir-Fry Chinese Chofu and Vegetables

Yield: 6 servings

This is the classic stir-fry, sophisticated enough to serve to company.

1 pound tofu, cut into ½-inch cubes

2 tablespoons canola oil

¾ cup sliced onion

¾ cup sliced celery

¾ cup sliced green bell pepper

¾ cup sliced carrot

1 cup Basic "Chicken" Broth, p. 44

1 teaspoon red pepper flakes

1 teaspoon garlic powder

3 tablespoons soy sauce

1 tablespoon cornstarch

2 tablespoons cold water

1 cup bean sprouts

6 cups cooked brown rice

1 cup crisp chow mein noodles

Stir-fry the tofu in 1 tablespoon of the oil for 2 minutes over high heat. Remove from the pan, add the remaining tablespoon of oil, and sauté the onion, celery, green pepper, and carrot for 3 minutes. Return the tofu to the pan, and add the broth, red pepper, garlic powder, and soy sauce. Cook for 3 minutes.

Dissolve the cornstarch in the water. Add it to the pan along with the bean sprouts, and cook, stirring constantly, until thickened. Serve over brown rice with a sprinkling of chow mein noodles.

Per Serving: Calories 161, Protein 11 g, Carbohydrates 10 g, Fat 7 g

Polynesian Chofu

Yield: 6 servings

This sweet-and-sour dish would also be good with fried tempeh chunks.

Whisk together all the sauce ingredients in a small bowl, and set aside.

In a large skillet or wok, heat the olive oil and stir-fry the garlic, onion, pepper, celery, and ginger for 3 minutes. Add the pineapple and almonds, and cook for 4 minutes.

Stir in the sauce ingredients, and cook until the sauce thickens. Add the prepared tofu and cook only until thoroughly heated.

Serve over brown rice.

Sauce:

1 cup unsweetened pineapple juice

2 tablespoons vinegar

2 tablespoons soy sauce

1 tablespoon cornstarch

1 tablespoon sweetener

2 teaspoons olive oil

1 clove garlic, minced

½ cup chopped onion

1 cup chopped green pepper

1 cup chopped celery

1 inch fresh gingerroot, grated

2 cups pineapple chunks

2 tablespoons slivered almonds

1 pound Teriyaki Tofu, p. 84

Per serving: Calories 211, Protein 8 g, Carbohydrates 30 g, Fat 6 g

Chofu with Eggplant

Yield: 6 servings

Spicy Chinese chili paste is a good condiment with this dish.

2½ pounds tofu, cubed

1 tablespoon olive oil

1 tablespoon tamari

1 large onion, finely chopped

2 garlic cloves, minced

2 cups peeled and cubed eggplant

2 cups chopped ripe tomato

¼ teaspoon marjoram

½ teaspoon dried basil

1 cup Basic "Chicken" Broth, p. 44

2 cups uncooked couscous

Sauté the cubed tofu in the oil and tamari until browned on all sides. Set the tofu aside and sauté the onion, garlic, and eggplant for several minutes until soft. Add the tomatoes, herbs, and stock. Cover and simmer over low heat for 30 to 35 minutes. Meanwhile, cook the couscous by adding to 4 cups boiling water. Stir just enough to make sure all of the grain is submerged. Remove from the heat, cover, and let sit for five minutes, then fluff with a fork to keep it from sticking together.

To serve, spoon the couscous onto a serving platter. Arrange the tofu on top of the couscous, and cover with the eggplant sauce.

Per serving: Calories 357, Protein 20 g, Carbohydrates 43 g, Fat 11 g

Chofu with Curry

Yield: 6 servings

This Indian curry couldn't be easier and makes a great "hurry-up" meal when time is short.

Sauté the tofu in the oil for 5 minutes, stirring constantly, until brown on all sides. Add the garlic, onions, and green pepper, and cook 3 more minutes. Add the curry powder and tomatoes, and stir well. Cover and simmer 15 minutes. Serve over rice with side dishes of one or two chutneys, chopped cilantro, and soy yogurt.

2 pounds tofu, cubed

2 teaspoons olive oil

2 cloves garlic, minced

⅔ cup chopped onions

½ cup chopped green pepper

1½ teaspoons curry powder

1½ cups chopped tomatoes

Per serving: Calories 157, Protein 11 g, Carbohydrates 9 g, Fat 8 g

My strongest experience on Bali had been to really be able to see, and identify with, a chicken.

— Alice Walker

Chofu Cacciatore

Yield: 6 servings

Using canned tomatoes makes this recipe a great quick-supper idea.

1½ pounds tofu, cubed

1 teaspoon olive oil

1 tablespoon garlic cloves, minced

½ cup white wine

1 cup vegetable stock

¼ cup tomato paste

1½ cups chopped tomatoes
(canned or fresh)

2 cups sliced mushrooms

2 tablespoons chopped fresh
parsley

½ teaspoon savory

1 teaspoon basil

½ teaspoon rosemary

½ teaspoon salt

¼ teaspoon black pepper

Simmer the tofu cubes in 2 cups water for 5 minutes, then drain.

Heat the olive oil in a large skillet, add the garlic, and sauté for 1 minute. Add all the remaining ingredients, stirring to dissolve the tomato paste. Bring to a boil, then cover and simmer for 15 minutes, stirring often. Uncover and continue to simmer for 10 minutes more. Add water if the mixture gets too thick. Serve over pasta.

Per serving: Calories 147, Protein 9 g, Carbohydrates 11 g, Fat 6 g

Creamy Chofu with Pasta

Yield: 6 servings

Reminiscent of creamed chicken favorites, this dish is particularly wonderful with spinach fettuccine.

Sauté the onion in the margarine or oil until golden, then add the bell pepper, mushrooms, and garlic. Cover and cook until the mushrooms are brown, 6 to 7 minutes. Stir in the flour and cook briefly, then whisk in the soymilk and cook until slightly thickened. Stir in the remaining ingredients, and heat thoroughly. Serve over pasta or rice.

— *from Jennifer Raymond*

1 onion, chopped

2 tablespoons dairy-free margarine or oil

½ bell pepper, diced

1 clove garlic, minced

3 cups sliced mushrooms

3 tablespoons flour

1½ cups soymilk

1 tablespoon finely chopped parsley

1 teaspoon salt

¼ teaspoon pepper

¼ teaspoon thyme

Pinch cayenne

½ pound firm tofu, crumbled

1 cup green peas

12 ounces pasta, cooked according to package directions

Per serving: Calories 206, Protein 9 g, Carbohydrates 25 g, Fat 7 g

Chickenless á la King

Yield: 6 servings

Even mushrooms can stand in for chicken, as this recipe demonstrates deliciously!

3 cups chopped mushrooms

1½ cup chopped onions

1 cup chopped carrots

2 cups chopped green peppers

1 cup flour

1½ cups peas

¼ cup tamari

3 cups soymilk

4 ounces pimento, chopped

In a large pan, steam the mushrooms, onions, carrots, and green pepper in ½ cup water for 5 minutes. Shake the flour and 1½ cups water in a jar until the flour is dissolved. Add to the pan with the vegetables. Stir in the peas, tamari, and soymilk. Cook over medium heat, stirring until the sauce thickens. Add the pimento and stir about 2 minutes. Serve over rice or baked potatoes.

Per serving (without rice or other side dish):
Calories 207, Protein 9 g, Carbohydrates 31 g, Fat 5 g

After a day of work I find such serenity sitting on the back porch watching my 5-year-old feed the chickens. I just take in the pastoral scene. It is poetry, it is beauty, and I am one of the lucky ones who has an opportunity to view it.

— Jeri Metz

Savory Scrapple

Yield: 6 servings

This is a traditional Pennsylvania Dutch recipe made from savory cornmeal mush that has been cooled until sliceable, then fried. It can be served for breakfast, as well as supper.

Sauté the onions and garlic in the margarine, stirring constantly, for 5 minutes. Add the cornmeal, thyme, sage, pepper, and salt, and stir well. Slowly whisk in the broth, stirring until smooth.

While continuing to stir, bring to a boil over medium heat. Lower the heat and cook for 15 minutes, stirring often.

Squeeze any excess water out of the tofu, and either crumble it into small pieces or chop it in a food processor. Mix the tofu into the cornmeal paste, and press the mixture into a well-oiled loaf pan. Chill for at least 4 hours. Remove from the pan and cut into ½-inch slices. Dip in flour and fry in oil, turning once until brown on both sides.

¾ cup finely chopped onions

2 teaspoons minced fresh garlic

1 tablespoon dairy-free margarine

1¼ cups cornmeal

½ teaspoon dried thyme

½ teaspoon dried sage

¼ teaspoon pepper

½ teaspoon salt

3 cups Basic "Chicken" Broth, p. 44

1 pound tofu, frozen and thawed

Flour, for dredging

Oil, for frying

Per serving: Calories 258, Protein 10 g, Carbohydrates 30 g, Fat 9 g

Quiche

Yield: 8 servings

This quiche is simple and wonderful. It's a meal in itself. The best vegetarian ham for using in this recipe is vegetarian Canadian bacon or frozen vegetarian ham logs.

2 (12.3 ounce) packages extra-firm silken tofu

¼ cup water

4¼ teaspoons Ener-G Egg Replacer powder

3 tablespoons nutritional yeast flakes

½ teaspoon turmeric

1 cup chopped onion

½ cup chopped bell pepper

1 tablespoon canola oil

1 cup shredded soy cheddar

1 cup chopped vegetarian ham (optional)

1 teaspoon fresh chives

Salt and pepper, to taste

One 9-inch flaky pie crust

Preheat the oven to 350°F.

Blend tofu, water, egg replacer, yeast, and turmeric in a food processor or in 2 batches in a blender until smooth.

Sauté the onion and pepper in the oil until soft. Mix into the tofu mixture with shredded soy cheddar, vegetarian ham, and seasonings, and pour into the pie crust. Bake for 50 to 60 minutes. Sprinkle with nutmeg and let cool 15 minutes before serving. This is also good cold.

Variations:

Instead of or along with the vegetarian ham, add 2 cups chopped fresh spinach, 2 cups sliced mushrooms, or 2 cups ground or sliced vegetarian sausage. Add ⅛ cup more water if needed. For the works, combine 2½ to 3 cups of all of these, or your choice of ingredients, to the filling.

— *from Nancy Robinson and Renee Wheeler*

Per Serving: Calories 211, Protein 10 g, Carbohydrates 15 g, Fat 11 g

Spinach Soufflé

Yield: 4 servings

Foregoing eggs doesn't have to mean giving up the delicious, light flavor of your favorite soufflé.

Preheat the oven to 350°F.

Thaw the frozen spinach, reserving the juice. Sauté the onions in 2 tablespoons of the oil until limp. Stir in the flour, liquid, ½ teaspoon salt, pepper, and nutmeg. Fold the spinach into the sauce. Blend the tofu, remaining 2 tablespoons oil, 1 teaspoon salt, lemon juice, and more black pepper until smooth and creamy. Fold into the spinach and sauce. Bake in an oiled 8-inch round pan or square pan for 30 minutes.

— *from Louise Hagler*
Tofu Cookery

1 (10-ounce) package frozen chopped spinach

½ cup chopped onions

2 tablespoons oil

3 tablespoons flour

1 cup liquid (including spinach juice and water, or soymilk)

½ teaspoon salt

Dash of freshly ground black pepper

Dash of nutmeg

1 cup tofu

2 tablespoons oil

1 teaspoon salt

2 tablespoons fresh lemon juice or vinegar

Dash of freshly ground black pepper

Per serving: Calories 214, Protein 6 g, Carbohydrates 11 g, Fat 15 g

Grilled Dishes

Instead of Chicken

Instead of Turkey

Grilled Chofu with Miso

Yield: 4 servings

Convert nonvegetarians at your next barbecue with this tempting recipe.

¼ cup dark miso

2 teaspoons sherry

1 tablespoon sugar

1 teaspoon grated fresh gingerroot

½ teaspoon crushed chili pepper

1½ pounds firm tofu

In a small bowl, combine the miso, sherry, sugar, ginger, and pepper with 1 tablespoon water to make a thick paste. Cut the tofu in ½-inch slabs. Grill over hot coals until browned on both sides. Brush with the miso sauce, and continue to grill for several minutes. Serve while hot.

Per serving: Calories 180, Protein 14 g, Carbohydrates 11 g, Fat 8 g

As each chick emerges from its shell in the dark cave of feathers underneath its mother, it lies for a time like any newborn creature, exhausted, naked, and extremely vulnerable. As the mother may be taken as the epitome of motherhood, so the newborn chick may be taken as an archetypal representative of babies of all species, human and animal alike, just brought into the world.

— Page Smith

Chofu Vegetable Shish Kebab

Yield: 6 servings

If you use bamboo skewers, be sure to soak them for 10 minutes in cold water before assembling these shish kebabs to help keep the skewers from charring.

Mix together the vinegar, oil, tamari, red wine, garlic, oregano, basil, and black pepper for a marinade. Pour this marinade over the tofu and vegetables, and cover, allowing everything to soak for 2 to 3 hours.

Skewer the tofu and vegetables pieces. Place on the grill and turn occasionally. Cook until the vegetables are done to your taste and the tofu is browned, about 15 to 30 minutes.

1¼ cups vinegar

½ cup oil

¼ cup tamari

3 tablespoons red wine

2 cloves garlic, crushed

½ teaspoon oregano

½ teaspoon basil

¼ teaspoon black pepper

2 pounds frozen tofu, thawed, squeezed, and cut into chunks

18 whole mushrooms

2 onions, halved and separated

2 zucchini, thickly sliced

2 sweet peppers, cut into bite-sized squares

18 cherry tomatoes

Per serving: Calories 353, Protein 14 g, Carbohydrates 17 g, Fat 23 g

Indian Tandoori Grill

Yield: 4 to 6 servings

This is a dairy- and poultry-free version of the traditional combination of yogurt, spices, and chicken which is cooked at very high temperatures in an Indian oven called a "tandoor."

1 (12.3 ounce) box soft silken tofu

2 tablespoons lemon juice

1½ tablespoons tandoori spice mixture*

1 pound chicken-style seitan

1 pound assorted vegetables, suitable for grilling (e.g., tomatoes, eggplant, zucchini)

2 large onions, sliced

3 tablespoons canola oil

Available in Indian grocery stores, natural food stores, and the gourmet or ethnic food sections of the supermarket.

Purée the tofu, lemon juice, and tandoori spice mix in a food processor. Cut the seitan and vegetables into chunks large enough to put on a skewer, and marinate in the tofu marinade from 1 to 24 hours in the refrigerator. Place the chunks on skewers that have been soaked in cold water for 10 minutes to reduce charring. Brown under an over broiler or grill until browned on all sides, turning as necessary. Meanwhile, sauté the sliced onions in the oil until soft and golden brown. Top the grilled vegetables and seitan with the sautéed onions. Serve with naan (an Indian flat bread), basmati rice, and chutney.

— *from Lynn Halpern*

Per Serving: Calories 258, Protein 20 g, Carbohydrates 11 g, Fat 21 g

Cilantro Sauce

Yield: 1½ cups

This makes a delicious chutney, good with Indian food, tofu cutlets, and chicken-style nuggets.

Combine all the ingredients in a bowl, and mix well.

1 cup finely chopped fresh parsley

2 cups chopped fresh cilantro

2 tablespoons finely minced fresh garlic

¼ cup red wine vinegar

2 tablespoons lemon juice

½ cup olive oil

Salt, to taste

Per tablespoon: Calories 44, Protein 0 g, Carbohydrates 1 g., Fat 4 g

It is one of those moments that will be engraved on my brain forever. For I really saw her. She was small and gray, flecked with black; so were her chicks. She had a healthy red comb and quick, light brown eyes. She was that proud, chunky chicken shape that makes one feel always that chickens, and hens especially, have personality and will. Her steps were neat and quick and authoritative; and though she never touched her chicks it was obvious she was shepherding them along. She clucked impatiently when, our feet falling ever nearer, one of them, especially self-absorbed and perhaps hardheaded, ceased to respond.

— Alice Walker

107

Stuffings
and side dishes

Instead of Chicken

Instead of Turkey

Wild Rice and Mushroom Stuffing

Yield: 6 to 8 servings

Wild rice is actually the product of a long-grain march grass grown around the northern Great Lakes region, and not a true rice. It's expensive, but can be easily combined with other grains and vegetables so that its distinctive flavor can be enjoyed more often.

1 cup uncooked, long-grain white rice

1 cup uncooked wild rice

4 cups Basic "Chicken" Broth, p. 44

1 cup chopped celery

1 cup chopped onions

3 cups chopped mushrooms

2 tablespoons dairy-free margarine

½ cup coarsely chopped toasted pecans

½ cup chopped fresh parsley

1 tablespoon soy sauce

1 teaspoon dried thyme

½ teaspoon dried sage

1 teaspoon celery seed

1 teaspoon dried savory

½ teaspoon black pepper

In a tightly covered pot, cook the rice and broth for 25 minutes until all the liquid is absorbed.

Preheat the oven to 350°F.

Meanwhile, sauté the celery, onions, and mushrooms in the margarine until just soft. Add to the cooked rice and mix thoroughly with the pecans, herbs, and spices. Bake in a covered, oiled casserole dish about 25 minutes until completed heated through.

Per serving: Calories: 278, Protein: 7 g, Carbohydrates: 38 g, Fat: 10 g

Michael's Mashed Potatoes

Yield: 6 servings

Mashed potatoes don't have to be the plain background for gravy, but can have an identity all their own.

Simmer the diced potatoes in enough water to cover for 15 minutes until soft.

In a skillet, sauté the peppers, celery, and garlic in the oil for 5 minutes. Add the tamari, dill, and basil, and cook for 3 minutes more.

Mash the drained potatoes and combine with the sautéed vegetables and tahini dressing. Beat until smooth and creamy.

7 large potatoes, diced

1 cup diced green pepper

1 cup diced celery

3 garlic cloves, minced

1 tablespoon oil

¼ cup tamari

1 teaspoon dried dill

1 teaspoon basil

½ cup Tahini Dressing, p. 112

Per serving: Calories: 203, Protein: 4 g, Carbohydrates: 35 g, Fat: 4 g

Tahini Dressing

Yield: 2 cups

Keep this on hand to add to mashed potatoes, as well as to use as the basis for tasty salad dressings.

¾ cup water

⅔ cup tahini

2 cloves fresh garlic, chopped

½ teaspoon paprika

½ teaspoon basil

1 teaspoon crushed dill

2 tablespoons diced onion

2 tablespoons lemon juice

2 tablespoons tamari

Process all the ingredients together in a blender until smooth.

Per tablespoon: Calories: 32, Protein: 1 g, Carbohydrates: 1 g., Fat: 2 g

Mila's Mashed Potatoes

Yield: 5 servings

Nutritional yeast helps replace the rich flavor of butter in this family favorite. Serve with Bantu's Brown Gravy, p. 44.

6 potatoes, peeled and cubed

2 tablespoons dairy-free margarine

1¼ cups soymilk

2 tablespoons nutritional yeast flakes

2 tablespoons chopped fresh parsley

½ teaspoon salt

Pepper, to taste

Simmer the potatoes in enough water to cover until soft. Drain and mash until smooth. Add the other ingredients and mix well.

Per serving: Calories: 209, Protein: 4 g, Carbohydrates: 35 g, Fat: 5 g

Our turkey, Guinevere, is especially fond of flute music. One day just after I had given her and Arthur some fresh greens, a flute solo came on the radio in the kitchen. Guinevere stopped eating, came to the foot of the stairs, and began a sweet trilling. She swayed from side to side in time with the music. When the music stopped, she went back to her bowl of greens.

— Marion Cleeton

Sweet Potato Stuffing

Yield: 6 servings

In this Southern favorite, sweet potatoes supplement the more traditional stuffing standard of bread crumbs.

5 sweet potatoes

2 tablespoons dairy-free margarine

1 cup chopped green onions

½ cup orange juice

1 cup plus 2 tablespoons fresh whole wheat bread crumbs

2 tablespoons chopped fresh parsley,

½ teaspoon salt

¼ teaspoon pepper

Peel the sweet potatoes, chop into chunks, and boil until tender, about 20 minutes. Drain off the water and mash by hand or in a food processor with 1 tablespoon of the margarine.

Preheat the oven to 350°F.

Sauté the green onions in the remaining tablespoon margarine for 2 minutes. In a baking dish, combine the mashed potatoes, sautéed green onions, orange juice, 1 cup of the bread crumbs, parsley, salt, and pepper. Mix well.

Sprinkle the remaining 2 tablespoons bread crumbs over the stuffing, and bake 20 minutes, or until set.

Per serving: Calories: 268, Protein: 4 g, Carbohydrates: 53 g, Fat: 5 g

Holiday Stuffing Casserole

Yield: 3 quarts (12 servings)

This dish that can be made the day before the feast. Serve with Bantu's Brown Gravy, p. 44.

Preheat the oven to 300°F.

Spread the bread cubes on a cookie sheet, and bake about 15 minutes to dry out but not brown. At the same time, roast the chopped pecans, also for about 15 minutes. Simmer the tempeh, bay leaf, and 1 cup of the stock for 15 minutes.

Cool the tempeh and dice. Sprinkle the tempeh with the tamari, then brown lightly in a hot skillet with 2 tablespoons of the oil. Add the onions, celery, and apples and remaining 2 tablespoons oil. Cook 5 minutes, then cover the pan and cook 5 minutes more.

In a large bowl, mix together the bread crumbs, fried tempeh, onion, celery, apples, roasted pecans, seasonings, and parsley. Pour the remaining 1½ cups stock over this mixture. When well mixed, pack the stuffing into a large, oiled baking dish. Cover the pan with foil, and bake for 30 minutes. Uncover and bake for 15 minutes more.

— *from Dorothy R. Bates*
The Tempeh Cookbook

8 cups bread cubes

½ cup chopped pecans

8 ounces tempeh, cut in half

1 bay leaf

2 ½ cups vegetable stock

2 tablespoons tamari

4 tablespoons oil

1 cup chopped onions

1 cup chopped celery

2 large tart apples, peeled and chopped

½ teaspoon each sage, thyme, marjoram, and mace

¼ cup minced fresh parsley

Per serving: Calories: 217, Protein: 7 g, Carbohydrates: 26 g, Fat: 9 g

Fruited Cornbread Stuffing

Yield: 8 servings

Cornbread stuffing finds its way onto many Southern tables at holiday time, and this fruit-rich recipe is as nutritious as it is delicious.

½ cup chopped dried apricots

½ cup chopped prunes

2 tablespoons raisins

2 teaspoons grated orange rind

½ teaspoon cinnamon

1 cup orange juice

½ cup Basic "Chicken" Broth,
    p. 44, or water

2 crisp apples, chopped

2 cups chopped celery

1½ cups chopped onions

3 tablespoons dairy-free margarine

1 cup chopped pecans

6 cups corn bread crumbs

Bring the apricots, prunes, raisins, orange rind, cinnamon, orange juice, and broth to a boil in a saucepan. Then turn off the heat, cover, and let sit for 10 minutes. Sauté the apples, celery, and onions in the margarine for 10 minutes until soft:

Preheat the oven to 375°F.

Combine the soaked dried fruit and sautéed vegetables with the chopped pecans and bread crumbs.

Bake in a covered, oiled baking dish for 20 minutes.

Per serving: Calories: 383, Protein: 6 g, Carbohydrates: 51 g, Fat: 16 g

Brazilian Rice with Coconut Milk

Yield: 6 to 8 servings

Serve this with a zesty black bean soup topped with orange slices.

In a heavy pot, sauté the onion in the oil until soft. Add the rice and cook for 2 to 3 minutes, stirring to prevent browning. Add the coconut milk, broth, raisins, and salt. Bring to a boil, then lower to a simmer, cover, and cook on a very low heat until the rice has absorbed all the liquid, about 20 minutes. Cover and allow to stand for 15 to 30 minutes before serving.

¾ cup finely chopped onion

2 teaspoons oil

2½ cups uncooked short-grained rice

2 cups unsweetened coconut milk

3 cups Basic "Chicken" Broth, p. 44, or water

1 cup raisins

¼ teaspoon salt

Per serving: Calories: 456, Protein: 6 g, Carbohydrates: 65 g, Fat: 17 g

Fried Basmati Rice

Yield: 6 servings

Be sure to add the liquid slowly to the sautéed rice, as it will splatter at first.

2 tablespoons dairy-free margarine

1 teaspoon cumin seeds

1 teaspoon cinnamon

1 teaspoon cardamom

1½ cups uncooked basmati rice, rinsed

½ teaspoon salt

3 cups water

Melt the margarine on medium heat, and add the cumin seeds. Stir until slightly browned. Add the cinnamon, cardamom, rice, and salt, and fry for several minutes while stirring. Slowly add the water, bring to a boil, then turn the heat to low. Cover the pot with a tight-fitting lid, and cook until all the water is absorbed, about 15 minutes. Check to see if the rice is done; cook for a few more minutes if there is still water in the pot, or add a little more water and cook if the rice in the middle is still tough. Cover and let sit before serving. Serve warm.

Per serving: Calories: 149, Protein: 3 g, Carbohydrates: 25 g, Fat: 5 g

Nasi Minyak (Scented Rice)

Yield: 6 servings

This Indonesian rice makes a nice accompaniment to grilled dishes.

Heat the oil in a deep pan. On medium-high heat, sauté the garlic, scallions, and ginger for a few minutes. Add the other spices and the rinsed rice, and fry 2 to 3 minutes until the grains begin to brown. Add the broth and salt. Bring to a boil, then lower to a simmer. Cover the pan and cook until the liquid is absorbed, about 15 to 18 minutes. Turn off the heat, cover, and let stand for 10 minutes before serving. Garnish with the raisins and serve hot.

2 tablespoons oil

3 cloves garlic, minced

6 scallions, finely chopped

1 tablespoon shredded fresh gingerroot

1 teaspoon cinnamon

½ teaspoon coriander

¼ teaspoon ground cloves

2 cups uncooked long-grained rice, rinsed

4 cups Basic "Chicken" Broth, p. 44, or water

¼ teaspoon salt

⅓ cup golden raisins

Per serving: Calories: 317, Protein: 7 g, Carbohydrates: 53 g, Fat: 9 g

Outstanding Stuffing

Yield: 4 cups

Your guests will remember this stuffing. This is my version of a distinctive South American recipe that's used to stuff huge cheeses. It's called Keshi Yena. Use it for stuffing mushrooms, potatoes, peppers, onions, squash, pasta shells, pastries, tofu turkey, vegetarian ham rolls, . . . it's endless!

¾ cup chopped onions

1 tablespoon dairy-free margarine

1½ cups chopped tomato

½ cup grated soy cheddar cheese

1 tablespoon dill pickle relish

½ cup toasted bread crumbs

1 (5.5 ounce) package mock ham slices, diced (Canadian bacon is best)

¼ cup chopped black olives

Egg replacer to equal 1 egg, p. 12

⅛ cup raisins

Dash of black pepper

Preheat the oven to 350°.

Sauté the onions in the margarine, then mix with the other ingredients.

Spread into an oiled 1-quart baking dish, and bake for about 20 minutes.

Outstanding Sweet Potato Stuffing: Mix the stuffing with 3 to 4 baked sweet potatoes, and serve in the potato shells. This should fill 6 to 8 halves.

— *from Nancy Robinson*

Per ½ cup: Calories 129, Protein 8 g, Carbohydrates 13 g, Fat 4 g

Desserts

Instead of Chicken

Instead of Turkey

Maple Tofu Cheesecake

Yield: one 8-inch pie (6 to 8 servings)

Chanticleer's Top Choice!

1½ pounds tofu, mashed

¼ cup oil

1⅓ cups maple syrup

Pinch of salt

One 8-inch pie shell

Preheat the oven to 350°F.

Process all the ingredients in a blender until smooth and creamy. Pour the mixture into an unbaked pie shell, and bake about 1 hour, or until set. Serve cold, topped with maple syrup and pecans or Sweet and Creamy Topping, below.

Per serving: Calories: 343, Protein: 8 g, Carbohydrates: 46 g, Fat: 13 g

Sweet and Creamy Topping

Yield: 1½ cups

Serve this as you would whipped cream

½ pound soft tofu

½ tablespoon lemon juice

¼ cup oil

2 tablespoons maple syrup

½ teaspoon vanilla

¼ teaspoon salt

Process all the ingredients in a blender until smooth and creamy, and chill.

— *from Louise Hagler*
Tofu Cookery

Per tablespoon: Calories: 31, Protein: 1 g, Carbohydrates: 1 g, Fat: 3 g

Chanticleer & Pertelote's Vanilla Cake

Yield: 6 to 8 servings

This is an easy recipe to double if you want a double-layered cake.

Preheat the oven to 350°F.

Sift the flour, baking powder, baking soda, and salt into a mixing bowl. Add the oil, liquid sweetener, water, and vanilla, and stir until smooth. Pour the batter into an oiled 9-inch cake pan. Bake for 25 to 30 minutes until done. Allow to cool before removing from pan. Top with your favorite frosting.

1½ cups whole wheat flour

½ teaspoon baking powder

½ teaspoon baking soda

¼ teaspoon salt

¼ cup canola oil

½ cup liquid sweetener

⅔ cup water

1 teaspoon vanilla extract

Per serving: Calories: 267, Protein: 4 g, Carbohydrates: 42 g, Fat: 9 g

Now the place was no longer strange to the Beautiful Pertelote, and she sang some clear, haunting melodies. Her singing was like the moon in a wintry night—sharp edges, hard silver, slow in its motion, and full of grace; so it took the place of much that was missing in those days, for there was no moon. And in this season of snow, Chanticleer and the Hen of the blazing throat were married.

— Walter Wangerin, Jr.

Triple Treat Cheesecake

Yield: 20 to 24 servings

When you remove the rim from your springform pan, you'll hear, "Oooh!" This cheesecake is the center of attraction at any gathering. Each layer is made from a basic recipe with flavors added. There are 5 main ingredients: dairy-free cream cheese, sugar, vanilla, egg replacer, and lemon juice. After a few times at this, you won't even need the recipe. This one is extra large and heavy.

1 dairy-free graham cracker crust

9 (8-ounce) packages dairy-free cream cheese

3 cups sugar

3 tablespoons vanilla

Juice of 3 lemon

3 tablespoons Ener-G Egg Replacer powder

Chocolate layer

¾ cup cocoa or melted chocolate chips

Strawberry layer

10 ounces frozen strawberries or 1 cup fresh strawberries (Save 5 for garnish.)

Start making this cheesecake 4 days ahead of serving.

Day 1—Chocolate layer: Tap the crust from the graham cracker crust pan into a 9-inch springform pan. Press down. Process 3 packages of the cream cheese, 1 cup of the sugar, 1 tablespoon of the vanilla, the juice of one lemon, 1 tablespoon of the egg replacer, and the cocoa or melted chocolate chips in a food processor (or in several batches in a blender) until smooth. Pour onto the crust, cover, and freeze.

Day 2—Strawberry layer: Make as for the chocolate layer, using the strawberries instead of the cocoa or chocolate chips. Process until just blended and pink; you might want some strawberry chunks in the filling. Pour over the chocolate layer, cover, and freeze.

Day 3—*Lemon layer:* Make as for the chocolate layer, using the lemon flavoring or juice instead of the cocoa or chocolate chips. Process until smooth, pour over the strawberry layer, cover, and freeze.

On serving day, thaw the cheesecake for about 4 hours. When the top layer starts to soften, place 2 to 3 rows of chocolate chips around the edge. Cut 4 fresh strawberries in half

Lemon layer

1 tablespoon lemon oil or lemon juice

lengthwise, and make an 8-petal flower in the center. Cut thin lemon slices once up to the center of the slice, twist, and place between the petals. Place 1 whole strawberry with its stem intact in the center.

— from Nancy Robinson

Per Serving: Calories 368, Protein 6 g, Carbohydrates 77 g, Fat 21 g

Lemon Frosting or Glaze

Yield: 1¾ cups

For chocolate or other cakes and desserts

Heat the margarine and milk together until the margarine melts. Stir in the sugar until smooth, then beat in the lemon juice and rind. Cool until thick enough to spread.

2 tablespoons dairy-free margarine

2 tablespoons soymilk or non-dairy cream

3 to 4 cups confectioner's sugar

3 tablespoons lemon juice

4 to 5 teaspoons grated lemon rind

Per 2 tablespoons: Calories 131, Protein 0 g, Carbohydrates 29 g, Fat 2 g

Cluck Cluck's Coconut Coffee Cake

Yield: 9 servings

If you've never used cereal in baking, you'll be surprised at the delicious results you'll get with this recipe.

½ cup bran cereal

1 cup coffee

1 tablespoon lemon juice

½ teaspoon vanilla

¼ cup canola oil

1½ cups flour

1 teaspoon baking soda

1 teaspoon cinnamon

¼ teaspoon salt

⅔ cup brown sugar

⅓ cup dried coconut

Preheat the oven to 350°F.

In a large mixing bowl, combine the bran cereal with the wet ingredients. Mix well. Sift in the dry ingredients and all but 2 tablespoons of the coconut. Pour into an oiled 8-inch square baking pan. Sprinkle the remaining coconut on top, and bake for 25 minutes.

Per serving: Calories: 285, Protein: 3 g, Carbohydrates: 43 g, Fat: 11 g

Chocolate Wacky Cake

Yield: 9 servings

Made in the pan it's baked in, this couldn't be easier.

Preheat the oven to 350°F.

Sift and mix together the flour, sugar, baking soda, and cocoa in an unoiled 8-inch cake pan. Make 3 wells in the flour mixture. Put the vanilla in the first well, the vinegar in the second, and the melted margarine or vegetable oil in the third. Pour the water over all, and mix with a fork until the ingredients are entirely moist. Bake for 30 minutes, or until a toothpick inserted in the center of the cake comes out clean.

1½ cups flour

1 cup sugar

1 teaspoon baking soda

¼ cup cocoa

1 teaspoon vanilla extract

1 teaspoon vinegar

6 tablespoons melted dairy-free margarine or vegetable oil

1 cup water

Per Serving: Calories 224, Protein 3 g, Carbohydrates 35 g, Fat 7 g

Cock-A-Doodle Creme-Filled Crumb Cake

Yield: one 10-inch tube pan (12 servings)

First Layer

½ cup brown sugar
1 cup flour
½ teaspoon salt
½ cup chopped walnuts
¼ cup oil

Second Layer

1 pound tofu, crumbled
3 tablespoons oil
½ cup sugar
1 tablespoon vanilla
2 tablespoons flour
½ teaspoon salt

Third Layer

½ pound tofu, crumbled
1 cup sugar
½ cup oil
¾ cup water
3 tablespoons fresh lemon juice
½ teaspoon salt
2 cups flour
½ teaspoon baking soda
2 teaspoons baking powder
½ cup chopped walnuts
½ teaspoon cinnamon

Preheat the oven to 375°F.

Mix ingredients for the first layer together in a bowl until crumbly. Press this mixture into the bottom and sides of a 10-inch tube pan.

In a blender, process the ingredients for the second layer until smooth and creamy. Spread on top of the first layer in the pan.

For the third layer, process the crumbled tofu, sugar, oil, water, lemon juice, and salt, and set aside. Mix the flour, baking soda, baking powder, walnuts, and cinnamon together in a bowl. Stir the blended ingredients for the third layer into the flour mixture until there are no lumps. Spread this over the second layer, being careful not to stir the second and third layers together. Bake for 40 to 45 minutes. Let sit for 5 minutes, then loosen the edges and turn out onto a plate or platter. Cool 10 minutes before slicing.

Per Serving: Calories 452, Protein 8 g, Carbohydrates 49 g, Fat 24 g

Texas Raspberry Cake

Yield: 15 to 18 servings

Preheat the oven to 375°F.

Combine the flour and granulated sweetener in large bowl. In a heavy pan, heat ½ cup oil, 7 tablespoons cocoa, and water to boiling, stirring well. Add the hot cocoa mixture to the flour mixture. Mix the egg replacer according to the package directions,and stir the baking soda into the ½ cup soymilk and vinegar. Add the egg replacer, fat replacer or remaining oil, and vanilla to the soymilk mixture, and mix well. Add this to the flour mixture, and mix well again. Pour the batter into an oiled 9 x 13-inch cake pan. Bake for 25 to 30 minutes.

During the last 5 minutes of baking, heat the margarine, 4 tablespoons cocoa, and 6 tablespoons soymilk in a heavy pan until boiling, stirring frequently. Add the confectioner's sugar, raspberries, and chopped pecans. Pour the hot frosting over the hot cake, and spread evenly. Cool before serving.

Per Serving: Calories 402, Protein 3 g, Carbohydrates 59 g, Fat 16 g

2 cups flour

1½ cups granulated sweetener

½ cup oil plus either ½ cup Wonderslim Fat & Egg Replacer, or applesauce

7 tablespoons cocoa

1 cup water

Ener-G Egg Replacer for 2 eggs, or 1 banana, mashed

1 teaspoon baking soda

½ cup warm soymilk + 1 teaspoon vinegar

1 teaspoon vanilla

½ cup dairy-free margarine

4 tablespoons cocoa

6 tablespoons soymilk

1 pound confectioner's sugar

1 cup raspberries

1 cup chopped pecans

Lower Fat Variation: Use non-fat soymilk and ¼ cup oil plus ¾ cup Won-derslim. Omit nuts. (You have to use margarine for the frosting to work.)

— *from Renee Wheeler*

129

Streusel Top Coffee Cake

Yield: 9 servings

This traditional breakfast favorite needs no eggs to make it a treat.

¼ cup canola oil

Ener-G egg replacer equivalent to
    1 egg

½ cup soymilk

1½ cups flour

¾ cup sugar

2 teaspoons baking powder

½ teaspoon salt

Topping

¼ cup brown sugar

1 tablespoon all-purpose flour

1 teaspoon ground cinnamon

1 tablespoon melted dairy-free
    margarine

½ cup chopped nuts

Preheat the oven to 375°F.

Combine the oil, egg replacer, and soymilk. Stir together the dry ingredients, and add the soymilk mixture. Pour into an oiled 9 x 9 x 2-inch pan. Combine the topping ingredients and sprinkle over the cake batter. Bake for 25 minutes, or until a toothpick inserted in the center of the cake comes out clean.

— *from Lynn Halpern*

Per Serving: Calories 256, Protein 3 g, Carbohydrates 35 g, Fat 11 g

Grandmother Turkey Lurkey's Lemon-Walnut Cake

Yield: one 9 x 9-inch pan (8 to 10 servings)

Try a variety of liquid sweeteners in this cake, from brown rice syrup to maple syrup.

Preheat the oven to 350°F.

Combine the liquid ingredients in a medium mixing bowl. Sift the flour, baking powder, baking soda, and salt into the bowl. Add the walnuts and lemon rind, and stir well.

Pour the batter into an oiled 9 x 9-inch pan, and bake for 25 to 30 minutes. The cake is done when a toothpick inserted in the center comes out clean.

⅓ cup canola oil

⅔ cup liquid sweetener

¾ cup lemon juice

2½ cups pastry flour

1½ teaspoons baking powder

½ teaspoon baking soda

¼ teaspoon salt

½ cup chopped walnuts

1 teaspoon grated lemon rind

Per serving: Calories: 340, Protein: 5 g, Carbohydrates: 51 g, Fat: 12 g

Each evening I wait for my great-grandmother to come and feed the chickens and close the chicken house. We kiss the phlegmatic brown hens and blow kisses to the flighty white ones. I hug my old grey rooster.

— Ieva Cucinelli

Frosted Brownies

Yield: 1 dozen

Freezing actually makes this recipe better, more moist! I make it the night before, freeze, then cut the brownies into squares while frozen, and defrost half an hour or more before serving.

½ cup dairy-free margarine, softened

1 cup sugar

3 tablespoons oil

1 (12.3 ounce) package soft silken tofu

⅓ cup unsweetened cocoa powder

1 teaspoon vanilla extract

1⅓ cups flour

½ teaspoon baking soda

¾ cup coconut

1 cup chopped walnuts (optional)

1 cup semi-sweet chocolate chips

Preheat the oven to 350°F.

Combine the margarine, sugar, and oil in a food processor or electric mixer, and process until light and fluffy. Add the tofu and process again until smooth, then mix in the cocoa powder and vanilla. Combine the flour and baking soda; add them to the blended ingredients, and process again briefly. Pour into a bowl and add the chocolate chips, coconut, and nuts, if using. Pour into a lightly greased 9 x 12-inch baking pan. Bake for 20 to 25 minutes, until a toothpick inserted in the center comes out clean. Frost when cool. Top with more nuts or chocolate chips, if you like.

— *from Leslie Crane*

Per Serving: Calories 392, Protein 5 g, Carbohydrates 37 g, Fat 24 g

Brownie Frosting

Yield: 1½ cups

Cream the sugar and margarine together, then mix in the cocoa and vanilla. Gradually add the hot coffee or soymilk, enough to thin the mixture to a spreading consistency

— *from Leslie Craine*

Per 2 tablespoons: Calories 141, Protein 1 g, Carbohydrates 30 g, Fat 2 g

- 3 cups powdered sugar
- 2 tablespoons dairy-free margarine
- ¼ cup cocoa
- 1 teaspoon vanilla
- 2 to 3 tablespoons hot coffee or soymilk

Mocha Frosting

Yield: 1½ cups

Flavored instant coffees will give an interesting twist to this frosting.

Cream the margarine and sugar in a medium bowl. Add the remaining ingredients, and stir until smooth.

Per 2 tablespoons: Calories 153, Protein 0 g, Carbohydrates 34 g, Fat 2 g

- 2½ tablespoons soft dairy-free margarine
- 3 cups confectioner's sugar
- ¼ cup cocoa
- 1 heaping teaspoon instant coffee dissolved in 1 tablespoon hot water
- ½ teaspoon vanilla
- 2 to 4 tablespoons soymilk or water

Pumpkin Bars

Yield: 2 dozen bars

Make these for Thanksgiving get-togethers. Served on a yellow-rimmed platter, they make a bright presentation.

1 cup unbleached all-purpose flour

½ cup quick oats

½ cup granulated sweetener

½ cup dairy-free margarine,
  or ¼ cup WonderSlim

2 cups canned pumpkin

1 cup soymilk or soy cream
  cheese

Egg replacer equal to 2 eggs

¾ cup granulated sweetener

2 teaspoons pumpkin pie spice,
  (or 1 teaspoon cinnamon,
  ½ teaspoon ginger, and
  ¼ teaspoon cloves)

½ cup chopped pecans

¼ cup granulated sweetener

2 tablespoons dairy-free margarine

Preheat the oven to 350°F. Mix the flour, oats, ½ cup sweetener, and ½ cup margarine until the dough is crumbly. Press into a 13 x 9 x 2-inch pan or glass baking dish, and bake for 15 minutes. Leave the oven on.

Mix the pumpkin, soymilk, egg replacer, ¾ cup sweetener, and spices, and beat well. Pour into the crust and bake for 20 minutes. Leave the oven on.

Mix the pecans, ¼ cup sweetener, and 2 tablespoons margarine, and sprinkle over the filling. Bake 20 more minutes or until set. Cool before cutting.

Per bar: Calories: 148, Protein: 2 g, Carbohydrates: 20 g, Fat: 6 g

Sheehan's Lemon Bars

Yield: 24 bars

My 4-year-old friend Sheehan said that when he grows up he's going to marry me and take care of me. I said that's fine with me. He then said, "And will you make me some lemon bars?" I said that's the best offer I ever had. So here's to these lemon bars bridging our age differences.

Preheat the oven to 350°F.

Mix 1 cup of the cake mix with the oats. Cut in the margarine until crumbly. Spread ¾ of the crumb mix in the bottom of a greased and floured 9 x 9-inch pan.

Blend the rest of the cake mix, the egg replacer, lemon flavoring, and cream cheese in a food processor or electric mixer until well combined. Pour into a mixing bowl, and stir in the mandarin oranges. Spread the mixture onto the crumb crust, and sprinkle the remaining ¼ cup crumb mixture over the top.

Bake for 30 minutes or until the top is browned. Cool completely before cutting into bars, and refrigerate until cold before serving.

1 (18.5-ounce) box dairy-free lemon cake mix

½ cup rolled oats

3 tablespoons dairy-free margarine

2 (8-ounce) packages dairy-free cream cheese, softened

1 tablespoon Ener-G Egg Replacer powder

1 tablespoon lemon flavoring

Sugar, to taste

1 (10.5-ounce) can mandarin oranges, drained

— *from Nancy Robinson*

Per Serving: Calories 179, Protein 3 g, Carbohydrates 20 g, Fat 10 g

Mother Hen's Homestyle Spice Drop Cookies

Yield: eighteen 3-inch cookies

These soft, spicy cookies are delicious.

½ cup raisins

¼ cup crumbled tofu

½ cup soymilk

1 tablespoon vinegar

1 cup granulated sweetener

1 cup whole wheat pastry flour

2 tablespoons oat bran

½ teaspoon baking soda

1½ teaspoons cinnamon

¼ teaspoon ground ginger

Cover the raisins with boiling water, and let stand for 10 minutes; drain.

Process the tofu, soymilk, and vinegar in a blender until smooth. Pour into a large bowl, and add the sweetener. Let stand 5 minutes.

Preheat the oven to 350°F.

In a separate bowl, blend the flour, bran, soda, cinnamon, and ginger. Stir into the liquid mixture along with the drained raisins, and mix thoroughly.

Drop by tablespoonfuls onto an oiled cookie sheet. These cookies will spread while baking, so leave generous space between them. Bake for about 10 minutes until golden brown. Let cool 2 to 3 minutes before removing to a rack.

— from Jennifer Raymond

Per cookie: Calories: 99, Protein: 1 g, Carbohydrates: 22 g, Fat: 1 g

Ms. Ticklefeather's Pumpkin Spice Cookies

Yield: 36 cookies

These plump, moist cookies are made with a flaxseed and water purée to replace the eggs called for in the original recipe. Flaxseeds may be purchased in most natural food stores or from the sources on p. 159.

Preheat the oven to 350°F.

Mix the dry ingredients together, and set aside. Process the flaxseeds and water in a blender for 1 to 2 minutes until the seeds are in tiny pieces and the mixture has the consistency of raw egg. Add the oil to the flaxseed mixture, and blend again to mix. Add to the dry ingredients, along with the pumpkin, additional water, and raisins. Mix until just combined and no dry flour is left.

Drop by tablespoonfuls onto an oiled baking sheet. Bake about 15 minutes until lightly browned. Remove from the baking sheet with a spatula, and place on a rack to cool. Store in an airtight container.

— *from Jennifer Raymond*

3 cups whole wheat pastry flour

4 teaspoons baking powder

1 teaspoon salt

1 teaspoon baking soda

1 teaspoon cinnamon

½ teaspoon nutmeg

1½ cups granulated sweetener

4 tablespoons flaxseeds

1 cup water

½ cup vegetable oil

1 cup solid-packed canned pumpkin

½ cup water

1 cup raisins

Per cookie: Calories: 109, Protein: 2 g, Carbohydrates: 18 g, Fat: 3 g

Mr. Gobble-Good's Gingerbread Cookies

Yield: 3 dozen cookies

These uncomplicated cookies won't last long in your cookie jar.

½ cup boiling water

1 cup molasses

1½ teaspoons baking soda

3 cups sifted flour

2 teaspoons ground ginger

Preheat the oven to 350°F.

In a mixing bowl, combine the boiling water with the molasses and soda. Add the flour and ginger slowly until a soft dough is formed. Chill at least 15 minutes. Take out part of the dough, and roll out on a floured board. Cut with cookie cutters. Bake on an oiled cookie sheet for 8 minutes. Repeat with the remaining dough.

Per cookie: Calories: 64, Protein: 1 g, Carbohydrates: 15 g, Fat: 0 g

I recently acquired a young male turkey who has brought an incredible energy change to our land. He is like a blinding rainbow and I protect him fiercely. One day, he was struck by a large hawk and was so frightened when I found him he wrapped his neck around me as I carried him, his head peeking out of my hair at the back, while my husband opened gates for us.

— Irene Hanson

Pecan Pie

Yield: one 9-inch pie (8 to 10 servings)

A friend in North Carolina had so many pecans in her back yard, she paid someone to shell them. Luckily, I was there right after the shelling. This is my version of traditional pecan pie. I consider the traditional recipe too sweet for me, so I use non-dairy cream cheese instead of another cup of sugar.

Preheat the oven to 350°F. Combine the egg replacer, corn syrup, sugar, tofu, margarine, and vanilla, and mix well. Stir in the pecans and pour into the pastry shell.

Bake for 50 to 55 minutes, or until a knife inserted near the center comes out clean. If the pastry starts to burn around the edge before the pie is done, cover with a strip of aluminum foil.

Chocolate Pecan Pie: Cover the pie shell with chocolate chips, then add the pecan filling.

Ener-G Egg Replacer equal to 3 eggs (with no additional water)

½ cup corn syrup

½ cup sugar

1 cup firm silken tofu or soy cream cheese

2 tablespoons melted dairy-free margarine, or 1 tablespoon WonderSlim

1 teaspoon vanilla

1½ cups pecans

1 unbaked 9-inch flaky pie shell

Per serving: Calories: 375, Protein: 7 g, Carbohydrates: 37 g, Fat: 20 g

Priscilla's Creamy Rice Pudding

Yield: 6 servings

Rice pudding is a favorite comfort food that does not need eggs to be rich and creamy.

3 cups cooked rice

3 cups soymilk

3 tablespoons sweetener

1 tablespoon cinnamon

1 teaspoon vanilla

¼ teaspoon salt

1 cup raisins

Simmer all the ingredients together for 15 to 20 minutes in a heavy-bottomed saucepan. Stir occasionally until the pudding begins to thicken. Serve hot or cold.

Per serving: Calories: 258, Protein: 6 g, Carbohydrates: 52 g, Fat: 4 g

Ener-G Custard Tart Filling

Yield: 6 servings

This recipe highlights Ener-G Egg Replacer in something other than cake. You'll enjoy the results.

3 cups soymilk

⅔ cup sugar

3 teaspoons fruit pectin

Ener-G Egg Replacer equivalent to 3 eggs

2 teaspoons vanilla

Dash of nutmeg

Per serving: Calories: 258, Protein: 6 g, Carbohydrates: 52 g, Fat: 4 g

Heat the soymilk to just below boiling, then remove from the heat. Mix the sugar and pectin together, then stir into the milk along with the other ingredients while mixing vigorously. Keep mixing until very smooth. Pour into custard cups, sprinkle with nutmeg, and refrigerate until firm.

Orange-Vanilla "Custard"

Yield: one 9½-inch deep-dish pie pan (8 to 10 servings)

Be sure to read "Cooking With Tofu" on p. 13 before blending more than 1½ pounds tofu at a time.

Preheat the oven to 400°F.

Combine the tofu, juice concentrate, oil, vanilla, and salt in batches in a blender or food processor until smooth and creamy. Pour into a large bowl.

In a separate bowl, mix the sugar, flour, baking powder, and baking soda. Combine this with the tofu mixture in the bowl, and blend in 2 batches until smooth. After blending the batches, pour them into a well-oiled and floured deep-dish pie pan, and bake for about 30 minutes. Serve hot or cold. Slice with a sharp, wet knife. The texture becomes denser as it cools.

2 pounds tofu, crumbled

⅔ cup frozen orange juice concentrate, thawed

¼ cup oil

1 teaspoon vanilla

½ teaspoon salt

1 cup sugar

½ cup flour

1 teaspoon baking powder

¼ teaspoon baking soda

— *from Louise Hagler*
Tofu Cookery

Per serving: Calories: 298, Protein: 9 g, Carbohydrates: 39 g, Fat: 11 g

141

Eggless Nog

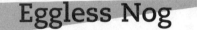

Yield: 8 servings

Turmeric will provide the golden color here instead of eggs.

2 (12.3 ounce) packages soft silken tofu

2 cups vanilla soymilk

1 tablespoon or more vanilla flavoring

¼ cup sugar

2 tablespoons brown sugar or Sucanat

¼ teaspoon turmeric

½ to 1 cup rum or brandy, or 1 teaspoon rum flavoring

Dash of nutmeg

Combine all the ingredients, except the nutmeg, in a blender, then chill. Sprinkle a dash of nutmeg over each cupful before serving.

—*from Nancy Robinson*

Per Serving: Calories 146, Protein 6 g, Carbohydrates 11 g, Fat 3 g

Holiday Menus

Instead of Chicken

Instead of Turkey

Farm Sanctuary's Thanksgiving Menu

(A favorite of farm animals everywhere!)

Chestnut Soup

Serves 6

Chestnuts are synonymous with the holiday season, showcased delightfully in this tasty soup.

2 pounds of chestnuts

1½ quarts rich soup stock

2 tablespoons dairy-free margarine

3 tablespoons flour

⅓ cup red table wine

¼ cup brandy

Salt, black pepper, and nutmeg, to taste

Dash of paprika

Preheat the oven to 350°F.

Cut a cross in the flat side of each chestnut with a sharp knife. Roast the chestnuts in the oven for 15 to 20 minutes. Remove them when they can be pierced easily with a skewer. Peel the chestnuts and grind finely in a blender or food processor. Combine with the stock in a medium saucepan, and simmer slowly for ½ hour. Melt the margarine in a soup pot, add the flour, and cook until brown, stirring constantly. Slowly add the hot soup, stirring well with a wire whisk. Add the red wine, brandy, and a little salt, pepper, and nutmeg. Simmer for 10 minutes, stirring often. Sprinkle with paprika and serve with crisp croutons.

Per serving: Calories: 312, Protein: 4 g, Carbohydrates: 55 g, Fat: 5 g

Cucumber-Tomato Salad

Yield: 6 servings

Lime juice gives this salad a nice change of pace.

Mix the cucumbers, tomatoes, onion, celery, and parsley together in a salad bowl.

Process the tofu, lime juice, sugar, salt, pepper, and oil in a blender or food processor until smooth.

Combine the vegetables and dressing, and serve.

4 cups sliced cucumbers

3 cups chopped tomatoes

⅔ cup chopped onion

1 cup chopped celery

½ cup chopped fresh parsley

½ pound tofu, mashed

3 tablespoons lime juice

1 teaspoon sugar

½ teaspoon salt

¼ teaspoon pepper

2 tablespoons oil

Per serving: Calories: 109, Protein: 4 g, Carbohydrates: 10 g, Fat: 6 g

Stuffed Acorn Squash

Yield: 6 servings

Try stuffing these little squashes instead of a turkey for your next holiday meal.

3 small acorn squashes

3 chopped green onions

1 tablespoon oil

1 cup diced celery

1 bunch coarsely chopped spinach

½ cup salted whole wheat bread crumbs

2 tablespoons dairy-free margarine

Preheat the oven to 400°F.

Halve and clean the squashes, and bake for 35 minutes. To make the stuffing, sauté the green onions in the oil until soft. Add the celery, cover, and cook on medium heat until soft. Add the spinach, and stir until it wilts. Stuff the squashes and sprinkle with the bread crumbs. Dot with the margarine and bake 10 to 15 minutes longer.

Per serving: Calories: 128, Protein: 2 g, Carbohydrates: 23 g, Fat: 2 g

Tofu Loaf

Yield: 6 servings

This is a great recipe for someone new to tofu.

Preheat the oven to 350°F.

Mix all the ingredients together in a large bowl. Grease the loaf pan with the oil, then press the mixture into the pan. Bake for about 1 hour. Let cool 10 to 15 minutes before removing from the pan. Garnish with more ketchup and chopped parsley, if you like.

1½ pounds (3 cups) tofu, mashed

⅓ cup ketchup

⅓ cup soy sauce

2 tablespoons Dijon mustard

½ cup chopped fresh parsley

¼ teaspoon black pepper

1 medium onion, finely chopped

¼ teaspoon garlic powder

1 cup whole wheat bread crumbs, rolled oats, or crushed corn flakes

2 to 4 tablespoons oil

Per serving: Calories: 183, Protein: 10 g, Carbohydrates: 12 g, Fat: 10 g

Purée of Yams

Yield: 6 servings

This recipe will fill your kitchen with delectable aromas.

5 large yams

½ cup orange juice

2 tablespoons grated orange rind

1 teaspoon grated fresh gingerroot

1 teaspoon cinnamon

1 teaspoon grated fresh nutmeg

1 teaspoon grated lemon rind

3 tablespoons chopped almonds

Preheat the oven to 350°F.

Cut the yams into large chunks. Combine the remaining ingredients in a blender, and process until creamy. Pour the blended mixture over the yams, and mix. Place the yams and purée into a baking dish, and sprinkle with the almonds. Bake for 25 minutes.

Per serving: Calories: 141, Protein: 1 g, Carbohydrates: 34 g, Fat: 0 g

Roasted Rosemary Potatoes

Yield: 6 servings

If you've never tried baking potatoes with fresh rosemary, you're in for a treat here.

Peel the potatoes, slice in half, and cook in boiling water for 10 minutes. Drain well. Preheat the oven to 375°F. Oil a shallow baking dish, and arrange a single layer of potatoes on the bottom. Pour the melted margarine over the potatoes. Sprinkle with the rosemary and ground pepper, and bake for 30 minutes, turning the potatoes occasionally.

6 medium potatoes

4 tablespoons melted dairy-free margarine

4 tablespoons fresh rosemary, or 2 tablespoons dried, crumbled rosemary

Freshly ground pepper, to taste

Per serving: Calories: 183, Protein: 2 g, Carbohydrates: 27 g, Fat: 7 g

Pecky, a tiny leghorn hen, is the most independent and shrewd. She dashes away from her flock as soon as their coop door is opened, and tries to roost in new and obscure places rather than with her companions. She protests indignantly when I scoop her up each night to put her inside the coop for protection, and gives me the impression that she is always measuring and assessing each new moment of her life.

— Holly Cheever

Wheat Berry Dinner Rolls

Yield: 24 rolls

These rolls provide the whole-grain nutrition of wheat berries.

1⅔ cups warm water

1 cup sprouted or cooked wheat berries

2 tablespoons powdered soymilk

1½ tablespoons active dry yeast

1 tablespoon brown sugar

1 tablespoon oil

1 tablespoon salt

5 cups whole wheat flour

Combine the water, wheat berries, and powdered soymilk in a blender briefly at medium speed. Pour over the yeast and brown sugar. After the yeast bubbles to the top of the liquid, add the oil, salt, and flour. Knead well until the dough is soft and elastic. Cover and let rise for 10 minutes. Knead again briefly. Pinch off 24 pieces and shape into rolls. Place in oiled baking pans lightly sprinkled with cornmeal, and let rise in a warm spot until doubled. Preheat the oven to 350°F, and bake for 15 to 20 minutes.

Per roll: Calories: 107, Protein: 4 g, Carbohydrates: 20 g, Fat: 1 g

Tofu-Pumpkin Pie

Yield: one 8 to 9-inch pie or one 10-inch tart (8 servings)

Tofu provides the custardy consistency that eggs traditionally impart to this holiday favorite.

Preheat the oven to 350°F.

To make the crust, mix together the flour, wheat germ, margarine, and salt. Add enough cold water to form a firm ball. Roll out the dough with a rolling pin, and place in a pie or tart pan. Set aside.

Process all the filling ingredients in a food processor or in batches in a blender until smooth, about 3 minutes.

Pour the filling into the crust, and bake for 45 minutes. Serve warm or chilled.

Crust:

1½ cups flour

¼ cup wheat germ

⅓ cup dairy-free margarine

½ teaspoon salt

4 tablespoons cold water

Filling:

1 (16-ounce) can pumpkin

1 pound tofu

½ teaspoon allspice

1 teaspoon cinnamon

1 teaspoon ground ginger

2 tablespoons canola oil

1 teaspoon vanilla

⅔ cup light brown sugar

¼ teaspoon salt

Per serving: Calories: 290, Protein: 8 g, Carbohydrates: 34 g, Fat: 13 g

Robin Goodfeather's Happy Holiday Menu

Stuffed Tofu Turkey

Yield: 8 servings

With this delicious stuffing and marinade, you'll never miss the bird.

5 pounds tofu

4 cloves garlic, minced

1 cup diced onions

1½ cups diced celery

1½ cups diced mushrooms

¼ cup sesame oil

½ cup minced fresh parsley

2 tablespoons garlic powder

1 tablespoon celery seed

2 tablespoons dried sage

1½ tablespoons dried savory

1½ tablespoons dried rosemary

1½ tablespoons dried thyme

1 teaspoon black pepper

½ cup soy sauce

4 cups soft bread crumbs

Line a 12-inch colander with a large piece of clean, damp cheesecloth. Crumble the tofu well, then pack it into the colander. Cover the tofu with overlapping cheesecloth, and place a dessert plate on top. Put a heavy object on top of the plate, and let rest for 1 hour at room temperature.

For the stuffing, sauté the garlic, onions, celery, and mushrooms in 1 tablespoon of the sesame oil. Add the herbs and half the soy sauce, cover, and cook 5 minutes, or until vegetables are soft. Add the bread crumbs and mix well.

Remove the weight and plate from the tofu, and open the top layer of cheesecloth. Scoop out the tofu with a large spoon, leaving 1 inch of the sides next to the colander. Press the stuffing into the hollowed tofu cavity. Cover the stuffing with remaining tofu, and press down firmly. Turn the stuffed tofu onto an oiled baking sheet, flat side down.

Preheat the oven to 400°F.

Combine the remaining sesame oil and soy sauce, and baste the tofu turkey with this mix. Cover the "turkey" with foil, and bake for 1 hour.

Transfer the "turkey" to a platter, and baste again. Garnish with parsley and serve with mushroom gravy and cranberry sauce.

Per serving: Calories: 361, Protein: 24 g, Carbohydrates: 20 g, Fat: 18 g

"Turkey" Gravy

Yield: 6 to 8 servings

A quick and easy accompaniment to the centerpiece of your turkey-free meal.

Sauté the mushrooms and onions in the oil until the onions are soft. Add the flour and cook until toasted, stirring constantly. Add the water and whisk together until smooth. Simmer on low heat for 15 minutes, stirring frequently to keep it from sticking.

6 cups sliced mushrooms

1½ cups chopped onions

2 tablespoons canola oil

¾ cup flour

7 cups water

Per serving: Calories: 104, Protein: 2 g, Carbohydrates: 14 g, Fat: 3 g

Sweet Potato Dressing

Yield: 6 servings

Try this as an alternative to traditional wheat bread or corn bread stuffings.

½ cup chopped celery

2 carrots, finely chopped

1 onion, finely chopped

2 tablespoons dairy-free margarine

2½ cups sweet potatoes, cooked and mashed

½ cup orange juice

1 teaspoon grated orange peel

¼ teaspoon ground allspice

½ teaspoon salt

Preheat the oven to 350°F.

Sauté the celery, carrots, and onions in the margarine for 5 minutes. Add the remaining ingredients and mix well.

Transfer to an oiled casserole dish, and bake for 30 minutes.

Per serving: Calories: 126, Protein: 1 g, Carbohydrates: 22 g, Fat: 5 g

Pumpkin Soup

Yield: 6 servings

No one will ever know that this sophisticated soup is this easy to prepare unless you tell them.

½ cup minced onion

1 tablespoon dairy-free margarine

1 (16-ounce) can pumpkin purée

3 cups soymilk

1 cup water

¼ teaspoon ground nutmeg

½ teaspoon salt

In a medium saucepan, sauté the onion in the margarine until tender. Stir in the remaining ingredients, and heat just to boiling, stirring constantly.

Per serving: Calories: 88, Protein: 3 g, Carbohydrates: 9 g, Fat: 4 g

Oatmeal Cookies

Yield: 2 dozen cookies

Now you can make this traditional favorite without eggs.

Preheat the oven to 350°F.

Cream the margarine and sugar, then add the egg substitute and soymilk. In another bowl, mix the oats, flour, baking soda, spices, and salt. Combine the two mixtures and mix well. Drop by teaspoonfuls onto greased cookie sheets, and bake for 12 to 15 minutes.

½ cup dairy-free margarine, softened

⅔ cup sugar

Egg substitute equivalent to 2 eggs

½ cup soymilk

3 cups rolled oats

1 cup unbleached flour

1 teaspoon baking soda

½ teaspoon ground allspice

½ teaspoon ground cinnamon

¼ teaspoon ground ginger

¼ teaspoon salt

Per cookie: Calories: 116, Protein: 3 g, Carbohydrates: 15 g, Fat: 5 g

Index

United Poultry Concerns, Inc.

dedicated to the Compassionate and Respectful Treatment Of Domestic Fowl

United Poultry Concerns is a national non-profit organization that addresses the treatment of domestic fowl in food production, science, education, entertainment, and human companionship situations.

As part of our mission, United Poultry Concerns operates a unique sanctuary for chickens and other domestic fowl in Machipongo, Virginia. We invite the public to visit us and see what a chicken can be when a chicken is free! United Poultry Concerns is also leading the way to replace school hatching programs with humane alternatives and to stop the cruel starvation of hens used for egg production known as "forced molting," and much more.

United Poultry Concerns publishes a quarterly newsletter, Poultry Press. We offer a variety of educational materials including *Prisoned Chickens, Poisoned Eggs: An Inside Look at the Modern Poultry Industry*, *Replacing School Hatching Projects*, *Replacing Eggs*, and *Instead of Chicken, Instead of Turkey: A Poultryless "Poultry" Potpourri*.

United Poultry Concerns is the only organization in the country and possibly the world exclusively devoted to the plight of domestic fowl. We are funded entirely by people who care and who want to make a difference for these birds—people like you. Please support us.

United Poultry Concerns
P.O. Box 150
Machipongo, VA 23405-0150
Ph: (757) 678-7875, Fax: (757) 678-5070
www.upc-online.org

Purchase these vegan books from your local bookstore or natural food store, or order from:

Book Publishing Co.
P.O. Box 99
Summertown, TN 38483
1-800-695-2241
(Please add $3.00 per book for shipping.)

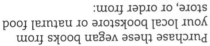

Prisoned Chickens, Poisoned Eggs
$12.95

Vegan Vittles
$11.95

The Uncheese Cookbook $11.95

Cooking with PETA
$14.95

Ingredient Sources

The Mail Order Catalog
P.O. Box 180
Summertown, TN 38483
800-695-2241, fax: 931-964-2291
catalog@usit.net
www.healthy-eating.com

A source for textured soy (including Chiken Brests™), Ener-G Egg Replacer, Mori-Nu Tofu, Tofu Scrambler, WonderSlim, seitan mixes, soymilk powder, tempeh starter, nutritional yeast flakes, Parmesan cheese alternative, and other meat and dairy substitutes — vegan cookbooks.